Bloom's Major Literary Characters

King Arthur

George F. Babbitt

Elizabeth Bennet

Leopold Bloom

Sir John Falstaff

Jay Gatsby

Hamlet

Raskolnikov and Svidrigailov

Bloom's Major Literary Characters

George F. Babbitt

Edited and with an introduction by
Harold Bloom
Sterling Professor of the Humanities
Yale University

CHELSEA HOUSE
P U B L I S H E R S
A Haights Cross Communications ✔ Company
Philadelphia

©2004 by Chelsea House Publishers, a subsidiary of
Haights Cross Communications.

A Haights Cross Communications ✦ Company

Introduction © 2004 by Harold Bloom.

Printed and bound in the United States of America.

10 9 8 7 6 5 4 3 2 1

Library of Congress Cataloging-in-Publication Data

George F. Babbitt / edited and with an introduction by Harold Bloom.
    p. cm — (Bloom's major literary characters)
Includes bibliographical references and index.
   ISBN 0-7910-7667-9
   1. Lewis, Sinclair, 1885–1951. Babbitt. 2. Lewis, Sinclair, 1885–
1951—Political and social views. 3. Satire, American—History and
criticism. 4. Businessmen in literature. 5. Conformity in literature.
6. Men in literature. I. Bloom, Harold. II. Major literary characters
III. Title. IV. Series.
  PS3523.E94B2945 2003
  813'.52—dc21

                       2003014154

Contributing editor: Sarah Robbins

Cover design by Keith Trego

Cover: ©Tom McCloskey, 2003

Layout by EJB Publishing Services

Chelsea House Publishers
1974 Sproul Road, Suite 400
Broomall, PA 19008-0914

www.chelseahouse.com

Contents

HAROLD BLOOM

The Analysis of Character

"Character," according to our dictionaries, still has as a primary meaning a graphic symbol, such as a letter of the alphabet. This meaning reflects the word's apparent origin in the ancient Greek character, a sharp stylus. *Charactēr* also meant the mark of the stylus' incisions. Recent fashions in literary criticism have reduced "character" in literature to a matter of marks upon a page. But our word "character" also has a very different meaning, matching that of the ancient Greek *ēthos*, "habitual way of life." Shall we say then that literary character is an imitation of human character, or is it just a grouping of marks? The issue is between a critic like Dr. Samuel Johnson, for whom words were as much like people as like things, and a critic like the late Roland Barthes, who told us that "the fact can only exist linguistically, as a term of discourse." Who is closer to our experience of reading literature, Johnson or Barthes? What difference does it make, if we side with one critic rather than the other?

Barthes is famous, like Foucault and other recent French theorists, for having added to Nietzsche's proclamation of the death of God a subsidiary demise, that of the literary author. If there are no authors, then there are no fictional personages, presumably because literature does not refer to a world outside language. Words indeed necessarily refer to other words in the first place, but the impact of words ultimately is drawn from a universe of fact. Stories, poems, and plays are recognizable as such because they are human utterances within traditions of utterances, and traditions, by achieving authority, become a kind of fact, or at least the sense of a fact. Our sense that literary characters, within the context of a fictive cosmos, indeed are fictional personages is also a kind of fact. The meaning and value of every character in a successful work of literary representation depend upon our ideas of persons in the factual reality of our lives.

Literary character is always an invention, and inventions generally are indebted to prior inventions. Shakespeare is the inventor of literary character as we know it; he reformed the universal human expectations for the verbal imitation of personality, and the reformation appears now to be permanent and uncannily inevitable. Remarkable as the Bible and Homer are at representing personages, their characters are relatively unchanging. They age within their stories, but their habitual modes of being do not develop. Jacob and Achilles unfold before us, but without metamorphoses. Lear and Macbeth, Hamlet and Othello severely modify themselves not only by their actions, but by their utterances, and most of all through *overhearing themselves*, whether they speak to themselves or to others. Pondering what they themselves have said, they will to change, and actually do change, sometimes extravagantly yet always persuasively. Or else they suffer change, without willing it, but in reaction not so much to their language as to their relation to that language.

I do not think it useful to say that Shakespeare successfully imitated elements in our characters. Rather, it could be argued that he compelled aspects of character to appear that previously were concealed, or not available to representation. This is not to say that Shakespeare is God, but to remind us that language is not God either. The mimesis of character in Shakespeare's dramas now seems to us normative, and indeed became the accepted mode almost immediately, as Ben Jonson shrewdly and somewhat grudgingly implied. And yet, Shakespearean representation has surprisingly little in common with the imitation of reality in Jonson or in Christopher Marlowe. The origins of Shakespeare's originality in the portrayal of men and women are to be found in the *Canterbury Tales* of Geoffrey Chaucer, insofar as they can be located anywhere before Shakespeare himself, Chaucer's savage and superb Pardoner overhears his own tale-telling, as well as his mocking rehearsal of his own spiel, and through this overhearing he is emboldened to forget himself, and enthusiastically urges all his fellow-pilgrims to come forward to be fleeced by him. His self-awareness, and apocalyptically rancid sense of spiritual fall, are preludes to the even grander abysses of the perverted will in Iago and in Edmund. What might be called the character trait of a negative charisma may be Chaucer's invention, but came to its perfection in Shakespearean mimesis.

The analysis of character is as much Shakespeare's invention as the representation of character is, since Iago and Edmund are adepts at analyzing both themselves and their victims. Hamlet, whose overwhelming charisma has many negative components, is certainly the most comprehensive of all literary characters, and so necessarily prophesies the labyrinthine complexities of the will in Iago and Edmund. Charisma, according to Max Weber, its first codifier, is primarily a natural endowment, and implies a primordial and idiosyncratic power over nature, and so finally over death. Hamlet's uncanniness is at its most suggestive in the scene of his long dying, where the audience, through the mediation of Horatio, itself is compelled to meditate upon suicide, if only because outliving the prince of Denmark scarcely seems an option.

Shakespearean representation has usurped not only our sense of literary character, but our sense of ourselves as characters, with Hamlet playing the part of the largest of these usurpations. Insofar as we have an idea of human disinterestedness, we tend to derive it from the Hamlet of Act V, whose quietism has about it a ghostly authority. Oscar Wilde, in his profound and profoundly witty dialogue, "The Decay of Lying," expressed a permanent insight when he insisted that art shaped every era, far more than any age formed art. Life imitates art, we imitate Shakespeare, because without Shakespeare we would perish for lack of images. Wilde's grandest audacity demystifies Shakespearean mimesis with a Shakespearean vivaciousness: "This unfortunate aphorism about art holding the mirror up to Nature is deliberately said by Hamlet in order to convince the bystanders of his absolute insanity in all art-matters." Of *Hamlet's* influence upon the ages Wilde remarked that: "The world has grown sad because a puppet was once melancholy." "Puppet" is Wilde's own deconstruction, a brilliant reminder that Shakespeare's artistry of illusion has so mastered reality as to have changed reality, evidently forever.

The analysis of character, as a critical pursuit, seems to me as much a Shakespearean invention as literary character was, since much of what we know about how to analyze character necessarily follows Shakespearean procedures. His hero-villains, from Richard III through Iago, Edmund, and Macbeth, are shrewd and endless questers into their own self-motivations. If we could bear to see Hamlet, in his unwearied negations, as another hero-villain, then we would judge him the supreme analyst of the darker recalcitrances in the selfhood. Freud followed the pre-Socratic Empedocles, in arguing that character is fate, a frightening doctrine that maintains the fear that there are no accidents, that overdetermination rules us all of our lives. Hamlet assumes the same, yet adds to this argument the terrible passivity he manifests in Act V. Throughout Shakespeare's tragedies, the most interesting personages seem doom-eager, reminding us again that a Shakespearean reading of Freud would be more illuminating than a Freudian exegesis of

Shakespeare. We learn more when we discover Hamlet in the Freudian Death Drive, than when we read *Beyond the Pleasure Principle* into *Hamlet*.

In Shakespearean comedy, character achieves its true literary apotheosis, which is the representation of the inner freedom that can be created by great wit alone. Rosalind and Falstaff, perhaps alone among Shakespeare's personages, match Hamlet in wit, though hardly in the metaphysics of consciousness. Whether in the comic or the modern mode, Shakespeare has set the standard of measurement in the balance between character and passion.

In Shakespeare the self is more dramatized than theatricalized, which is why a Shakespearean reading of Freud works out so well. Character-formation after the passing of the Oedipal stage takes the place of fetishistic fragmentings of the self. Critics who now call literary character into question, and who proclaim also the death of the author, invariably also regard all notions, literary and human, of a stable character as being mere reductions of deeper pre-Oedipal desires. It becomes clear that the fortunes of literary character rise and fall with the prestige of normative conceptions of the ego. Shakespeare's Iago, who wars against being, may be the first deconstructionist of the self, with his proclamation of "I am not what I am." This constitutes the necessary prologue to any view that would regard a fixed ego as a virtual abnormality. But deconstructions of the self are no more modern than Modernism is. Like literary modernism, the decentered ego came out of the Hellenistic culture of ancient Alexandria. The Gnostic heretics believed that the psyche, like the body, was a fallen entity, mechanically fashioned by the Demiurge or false creator. They held however that each of us possessed also a spark or pneuma, which was a fragment of the original Abyss or true, alien God. The soul or psyche within every one of us was thus at war with the self or pneuma, and only that sparklike self could be saved.

Shakespeare, following after Chaucer in this respect, was the first and remains still the greatest master of representing character both as a stable soul and a wavering self. There is a substance that endures in Shakespeare's figures, and there is also a quicksilver rendition of the unsettling sparks. Racine and Tolstoy, Balzac and Dickens, follow in Shakespeare's wake by giving us some sense of pre-Oedipal sparks or drives, and considerably more sense of post-Oedipal character and personality, stabilizations or sublimations of the fetish-seeking drives. Critics like Leo Bersani and René Girard argue eloquently against our taking this mimesis as the only proper work of literature. I would suggest that strong fictions of the self, from the Bible through Samuel Beckett, necessarily participate in both modes, the sublimation of desire, and the persistence of a primordial desire. The mystery of Hamlet or of Lear is intimately invested in the tangled mixture of the two modes of representation.

Psychic mobility is proposed by Bersani as the ideal to which deconstructions of the literary self may yet guide us. The ideal has its pathos, but the realities of literary representation seem to me very different, perhaps destructively so. When a novelist like D. H. Lawrence sought to reduce his characters to Eros and the Death Drive, he still had to persuade us of his authority at mimesis by lavishing upon the figures of *The Rainbow* and *Women in Love* all of the vivid stigmata of normative personality. Birkin and Ursula may represent antithetical and uncanny drives, but they develop and change as characters pondering their own pronouncements and reactions to self and others. The cost of a non-Shakespearean representation is enormous. Pynchon, in *The Crying of Lot 49* and *Gravity's Rainbow*, evades the burden of the normative by resorting to something like Christopher Marlowe's art of caricature in *The Jew of Malta*. Marlowe's Barabas is a marvelous rhetorician, yet he is a cartoon alongside the troublingly equivocal Shylock. Pynchon's personages are deliberate cartoons also, as flat as comic strips. Marlowe's achievement, and Pynchon's, are beyond dispute, yet they are like the prelude and the postlude to Shakespearean reality. They do not wish to engage with our hunger for the empirical world and so they enter the problematic cosmos of literary fantasy.

No writer, not even Shakespeare or Proust, alters the available stock that we agree to call reality, but Shakespeare, more than any other, does show us how much of reality we could encounter if only we retained adequate desire. The strong literary representation of character is already an analysis of character, and is part of the healing work of a literary culture, which implicitly seeks to cure violence through a normative mimesis of ego, *as if it were stable*, whether in actuality it is or is not. I do not believe that this is a social quest taken on by literary culture, but rather that we confront here the aesthetic essence of what makes a culture *literary*, rather than metaphysical or ethical or religious. A culture becomes literary when its conceptual modes have failed it, which means when religion, philosophy, and science have begun to lose their authority. If they cannot heal violence, then literature attempts to do so, which may be only a turning inside out of the critical arguments of Girard and Bersani.

I conclude by offering a particular instance or special case as a paradigm for the healing enterprise that is at once the representation and the analysis of literary character. Let us call it the aesthetics of being outraged, or rather of successfully representing the state of being outraged. W. C. Fields was one modern master of such representation, and Nathanael West was another, as was Faulkner before him. Here also the greatest master remains Shakespeare, whose Macbeth, himself a bloody outrage, yet retains our imaginative sympathy precisely because he grows increasingly outraged as he experiences the equivocation of the fiend that lies like truth. The double-natured promises and the prophecies of the weird sisters finally induce in Macbeth an apocalyptic version of the stage actor's anxiety at missing cues, the horror of a phantasmagoric stage fright of missing one's time, of always reacting too late. Macbeth, a veritable monster of solipsistic inwardness but no intellectual, counters his dilemma by fresh murders, that prolong him in time yet provoke him only to a perpetually freshened sense of being outraged, as all his expectations become still worse confounded. We are moved by Macbeth, however estrangedly, because his terrible inwardness is a paradigm for our own solipsism, but also because none of us can resist a strong and successful representation of the human in a state of being outraged.

The ultimate outrage is the necessity of dying, an outrage concealed in a multitude of masks, including the tyrannical ambitions of Macbeth. I suspect that our outrage at being outraged is the most difficult of all our affects for us to represent to ourselves, which is why we are so inclined to imaginative sympathy for a character who strongly conveys that affect to us. The Shrike of West's *Miss Lonelyhearts* or Faulkner's Joe Christmas of *Light in August* are crucial modern instances, but such figures can be located in many other works, since the ability to represent this extreme emotion is one of the tests that strong writers are driven to set for themselves.

However a reader seeks to reduce literary character to a question of marks on a page, she will come at last to the impasse constituted by the thought of death, her death, and before that to all the stations of being outraged that memorialize her own drive towards death. In reading, she quests for evidences that are strong representations, whether of her desire or her despair. Such questings constitute the necessary basis for the analysis of literary character, an enterprise that always will survive every vagary of critical fashion.

Editor's Note

My Introduction, while admitting the inadequacies of Sinclair Lewis as a novelist, nevertheless grants his distinction as an American mythmaker.

Russell Ames defends Lewis's caricatures for their rough truth, while the fierce H. L. Mencken salutes Babbitt for "his complete lack of originality."

The shrewd Rebecca West sees Babbitt as "a bonehead Walt Whitman," after which the noted short-story writer Sherwood Anderson dismisses Sinclair Lewis as one of the dreary spiritual dead.

Some redemption for poor Lewis is attempted by Stephen S. Conroy, who discovers in the maker of Babbitt a valid sociological imagination, while Dick Wagenaar documents Lewis's preference for Emersonian America over European retreat.

Bea Knodel measures the improvement in a woman's situation from the days of Lewis until our own, after which David G. Pugh measures Babbitt against T. S. Eliot, with not unexpected results.

Gore Vidal, amiably acidulous, gives us a rather melancholy overview of Lewis, while James M. Hutchisson describes how faithfully and factually Lewis fabricated his portrait of poor Babbitt.

Introduction

Can a Major Literary Character also be a Period Piece? I am inclined to utter a resounding "No!," but Babbitt may be something of a special case. I open the splendid *American Heritage Dictionary of the English Language, Fourth Edition* (Houghton Mifflin, 2000), and on page 128 find this entry:

> *Babbitt*, n. A narrow-minded, self-satisfied person with an unthinking attachment to middle-class values and materialism.

Joyce's Poldy Bloom and Marcel Proust's narrator (eventually called Marcel) are certainly not period pieces, but they have not become words, or at least dictionary entries. Did Sinclair Lewis, at least with Babbitt and Elmer Gantry, somehow capture the style of the age, 1922 to 1927? *The Waste Land* was published in 1922, and *The Hollow Men* in 1925. A world waiting for the blessed rain of Anglo-Catholicism is a certain distance from Mid-West America thirsting for a parody of the American religion, and yet Babbitt, if he had a touch more imagination, could reside amidst Eliot's stony images. Unlike Scott Fitzgerald, who overtly imitated Eliot in *The Great Gatsby*, Lewis was indifferent to Eliot, but Babbitt's book concludes with the chant of an unhappy man confronting the unlived life:

> "Well—" Babbitt crossed the floor, slowly, ponderously, seeming a little old. "I've always wanted you to have a college

degree." He meditatively stamped across the floor again. "But I've never—Now, for heaven's sake, don't repeat this to your mother, or she'd remove what little hair I've got left, but practically, I've never done a single thing I've wanted to in my whole life! I don't know 's I've accomplished anything except just get along. I figure out I've made about a quarter of an inch out of a possible hundred rods. Well, maybe you'll carry things on further. I don't know. But I do get a kind of sneaking pleasure out of the fact that you knew what you wanted to do and did it. Well, those folks in there will try to bully you, and tame you down. Tell 'em to go to the devil! I'll back you. Take your factory job, if you want to. Don't be scared of the family. No, nor all of Zenith. Nor of yourself, the way I've been. Go ahead, old man! The world is yours!"

Babbitt has gotten along—no more, no less. Still, he is neither a good hater like the anti-Semitic Eliot, nor a man of genius, again like Eliot. With all his narrow-mindedness, his boosterism, his smugness, he is not altogether a bad man.

RUSSELL AMES[1]

Sinclair Lewis Again

From a passionately democratic literary point of view it is a pity that so many of our social realists are clumsy, humorless fellows—sitting birds for critical buckshot. And so we must plead with Warren Beck,[2] Maxwell Geismar,[3] and other skilful hunters: "Can't you blast away at Sinclair Lewis when he's on the rise? Must you pepper him when he sits with a broken wing? Where's your sporting instinct? After all, he has pretty good company—Dickens, Whitman, Dreiser—better men of course—and in his own rank there are Whittier, Jack London, Upton Sinclair—limited, crude, wonderful writers. Thank God we get a Twain, a Gorki, a Lardner, a Berthold Brecht, once in a while—a people's satirist who really makes language behave."

And then a second thought may make us a little less apologetic. Granted that there are certain virtues of logic, coherence, and appropriateness that are almost absolute in literature—isn't our generation getting pretty narrow in its aesthetic? Haven't we become prisoners of a "new neoclassicism"—automatically, unconsciously humble before the flat purity of Hemingway or the petty subtlety of *New Yorker* fiction? If not this— aren't we too much awed by the seeming opposite to these barefoot sophisticates? Aren't we too humble before those who make no secret of the fact that theirs is a private symbolism—a code, a mystery, signals to the

From *College English* 10, Issue 2 (November 1948). © 1948 by the National Council of Teachers of English.

lonely fellow-hawk? Every poem a double play? From Joyce to Auden to Tate....

The trouble, we may say, with nearly every theory of art, is its narrowness or lopsidedness. Let us value the modern masters of sensitivity for giving us a sharp and brilliant vision of the surface of our lives (Hemingway, Mansfield), and for leading us into the unhappy caverns of our own minds (Mann, Kafka); but let us not ignore the coarse-textured realists, the story-tellers, the architects of our social consciousness (Lewis, Frank Norris), even when they ignore taste and grace. The novel, in its very origins, developed the bourgeois, prosaic view of life. It stripped the aristocracy of its knightly veils, its shimmering poetry (Rabelais, Cervantes). Its function, even in a great variety of specialized modern uses, has remained primarily prosaic—the study of man in the social web, or the study of the web itself. No other art form has the novel's freedom from selection, freedom for documentation of every aspect of the life of the individual. The epic, the play, the opera, the film—none of these can give us so completely, in general and in detail, that prose of life which is the novel's genius, its essence, its true function. From More's *Utopia* to *Gargantua and Pantargruel* to *Tom Jones* to *The Brothers Karamazov* to *Babbitt* moves the social and realistic impulse of the novel. Occasionally a *Wuthering Heights* goes off on a poetic kick, spends all its energy on its brilliant self, and has no successor.

We must permit, more or less, all of Warren Beck's judgment of Lewis' novels. *Main Street*, *Babbitt*, and *Arrowsmith* were his finest work; *Kingsblood Royal* probably belongs in a second-rate trio with *Dodsworth* and *It Can't Happen Here*; the remainder have been "perennially disappointing"; usually Lewis gives us caricature rather than character; there is not much dignity, subtle irony, or high comedy in him; he often writes badly and destroys fictional illusion; he falls below Dos Passos and Steinbeck, at their best, in breadth or power; he has no genuine tragic heroes in his books and few human beings of any high order; and, finally, it is true that "he had not the intuitive sympathy and artistic power to enhance Neil Kingsblood's story with a pity and terror potential in it." All this admitted, it seems impossible that Warren Beck should be wrong about Sinclair Lewis, but he is—not so much in what he says as in what he does not say.

Lewis, at his best, deeply enriches American art. His best books have the energy, the color, and the enduring force that belong only to the artist who has something new to say, who overcomes "cultural lag," who penetrates the shell of past life to lay bare the new life and the old decay that lie beneath. With unusual boldness, integrity, and faithfulness Lewis examined American character and culture, showing it as it is, as it has become, rather than as it used to be.

The primary *human* fact of modern history is the fact that specialization and commerce, since the Renaissance, have robbed the average individual of richness of life—craft skill, stability, close personal relations, property, and heroism. The Jeffersonian farmer was a revolutionary, a capitalist, a pioneer, a warrior. His successor today is, by comparison, a little man—Babbittish, routinized, timid, inert, platitudinous, commercial. What Veblen said to a few of us in his tortured Latinate prose, Lewis said clearly, to many, in a caricature of the American language. We would, of course, prefer to believe that we are still Patrick Henrys and Paul Bunyans—and it is fortunately true that their spirit, though sleeping, is not dead in us—but the main truth is otherwise: we have lost much; and Finley Peter Dunne and Lewis and Ring Lardner have not let us forget it.

If there is little that is dignified and heroic in Lewis' books, there has been little that is dignified and heroic in typical American life and less in our literature through half a century. Outside, or underneath, the dominant culture—in the lives of Negroes, lonely farmers, pioneering organizers of labor, millions of mothers fighting poverty—there has been dignity and heroism to spare. But it has found only occasional expression in a Ma Joad, a Tom Joad, a Preacher Casy. In what little there has been, Lewis has shared. His Leora, in *Arrowsmith*, is the most profound and sensitive characterization of a woman in all American literature, with a positive and poetical quality going beyond even Dreiser's Jennie Gerhardt. His Negroes in the very faulty *Kingsblood Royal* have dignity, warmth, courage, and healthy humor. Warren Beck says that "Lewis sentimentalizes the Negroes and caricatures the Caucasians," but the present writer is one white American who saw the contrast as essentially and shamefully true.

The severest restriction of Lewis' realism has been his focus upon the middle class, which extends even to the Negroes of *Kingsblood Royal*. The restriction has brought him some strength, of course, and Maxwell Geismar grants that Lewis' novels "form a remarkable diary of the middle-class mind in America." Geismar protests, however, that "surely the Middle-Class Empire is one of the most limited phases of the innumerable phases of history—and not only of world history but of American history...." The direct opposite is more nearly true. The central motif of modern history has been the centuries-long record of the magnificent and piddling exploits of the middle class. American history, except for the potent but defeated horror of slavery, is uniquely middle-class history. American character and culture, from top to bottom, has been soaked in middle-class ideas and ideals.

For Geismar the key to Lewis' work is knowledge of Lewis' personal identification with middle-class values. This is half true, and it does explain his failures. More important is Lewis' rejection of middle-class values, and this explains his successes. In Lewis we find self-criticism, not an everyday bourgeois virtue. Like nearly every other serious American writer of this century, from Twain and Henry Adams on down, he has felt the terrifying pressure of scientific determinism and of economic monopoly. He has responded negatively, with pessimism, and yet with an honest desire for democracy, individual growth, progress, and the social use of science. In *Kingsblood Royal* he has revealed some of the wretched sickness of America, whereas before he had dealt chiefly with the empty quality of a dominantly middle-class existence. This is an advance, artistically and intellectually—a remarkable advance late in a career. The contribution is negative rather than positive, but is a welcome sign of health and durability in the old tradition of American democratic individualism.

For a positive view of America today we must turn to writers like the Steinbeck of *Grapes of Wrath*—writers who occasionally draw close to that vision and understanding which Americans have been gaining from painful struggle throughout our history. To such a positive view there are few alternatives: the heroic exploits of clean-cut Anglo-Saxons in the dream-world of commercial fiction; or the despairing heroism of their artistically presented cousins, like Hemingway's Robert Jordan or one of Marquand's valiant aristocrats. In the latter there is much technical brilliance, subtlety, and self-conscious sensitivity; and Sinclair Lewis has little of these virtues; but his harsh caricature of our life has an honesty and rough truth of which much will endure when the falser and thinner fabric of finer writing has worn away. The pitifully groping and rebellious Carol Kennicott and George Babbitt will last; Martin Arrowsmith, the blundering creative modern Everyman, will last; above all lovely Leora Arrowsmith will last—because they have been brought clearly to our view, up through the appearances of the surface of life, out of the reality of struggling human life itself.

NOTES

1. Queens College, Flushing, N.Y.; author of *The Utopia of Citizen Thomas More*, to be published this winter by Princeton University Press.

2. "How Good Is Sinclair Lewis?" *College English*, January, 1948.

3. "Diarist of the Middle-Class Mind," *Saturday Review of Literature*, November 1, 1947.

H.L. MENCKEN

Portrait of an American Citizen

The theory lately held in Greenwich Village that the merit and success of *Main Street* constituted a sort of double-headed accident, probably to be ascribed to a case of mistaken identity on the part of God—this theory blows up with a frightful roar toward the middle of *Babbitt*. The plain truth is, indeed, that *Babbitt* is at least twice as good a novel as *Main Street* was—that it avoids all the more obvious faults of that celebrated work, and shows a number of virtues that are quite new. It is better designed than *Main Street*; the action is more logical and coherent; there is more imagination in it and less bald journalism; above all, there is a better grip upon the characters. If Carol Kennicott, at one leap, became as real a figure to most literate Americans as Jane Addams or Nan Patterson; then George F. Babbitt should become as real as Jack Dempsey or Charlie Schwab. The fellow simply drips with human juices. Every one of his joints is movable in all directions. Real freckles are upon his neck and real sweat stands out upon his forehead. I have personally known him since my earliest days as a newspaper reporter, back in the last century. I have heard him make such speeches as Cicero never dreamed of at banquets of the Chamber of Commerce. I have seen him marching in parades. I have observed him advancing upon his Presbyterian tabernacle of a Sunday morning, his somewhat stoutish lady upon his arm. I have watched and heard him crank his Buick. I have noted the effect of

From *Sinclair Lewis: A Collection of Critical Essays*, ed. Mark Schorer. © 1962 by Prentice Hall, Inc.

alcohol upon him, both before and after Prohibition. And I have seen him, when some convention of Good Fellows was in town, at his innocent sports in the parlors of brothels, grandly ordering wine at $10 a round and bidding the professor play "White Wings."

To me his saga, as Sinclair Lewis has set it down, is fiction only by a sort of courtesy. All the usual fittings of the prose fable seem to be absent. There is no plot whatever, and very little of the hocus-pocus commonly called development of character. Babbitt simply grows two years older as the tale unfolds; otherwise he doesn't change at all—any more than you or I have changed since 1920. Every customary device of the novelist is absent. When Babbitt, revolting against the irksome happiness of his home, takes to a series of low affairs with manicure girls, grass-widows and ladies even more complaisant, nothing overt and melodramatic happens to him. He never meets his young son Teddy in a dubious cabaret; his wife never discovers incriminating correspondence in his pockets; no one tries to blackmail him; he is never present when a joint is raided. The worst punishment that falls upon him is that his old friends at the Athletic Club—cheats exactly like himself—gossip about him a bit. Even so, that gossip goes no further; Mrs. Babbitt does not hear it. When she accuses him of adultery, it is simply the formal accusation of a loving wife: she herself has absolutely no belief in it. Moreover, it does not cause Babbitt to break down, confess and promise to sin no more. Instead, he lies like a major-general, denounces his wife for her evil imagination, and returns forthwith to his carnalities. If, in the end, he abandons them, it is not because they torture his conscience, but because they seem likely to hurt his business. This prospect gives him pause, and the pause saves him. He is, beside, growing old. He is 48, and more than a little bald. A night out leaves his tongue coated in the morning. As the curtain falls upon him he is back upon the track of rectitude—a sound business man, a faithful Booster, an assiduous Elk, a trustworthy Presbyterian, a good husband, a loving father, a successful and unchallenged fraud.

Let me confess at once that this story has given me vast delight. I know the Babbitt type, I believe, as well as most; for twenty years I have devoted myself to the exploration of its peculiarities. Lewis depicts it with complete and absolute fidelity. There is irony in the picture; irony that is unflagging and unfailing, but nowhere is there any important departure from the essential truth. Babbitt has a great clownishness in him, but he never becomes a mere clown. In the midst of his most extravagant imbecilities he keeps both feet upon the ground. One not only sees him brilliantly; one also understands him; he is made plausible and natural. As an old professor of Babbittry I welcome him as an almost perfect specimen—a genuine museum piece. Every American city swarms with his brothers. They run things in the

Republic, East, West, North, South. They are the originators and propagators of the national delusions—all, that is, save those which spring from the farms. They are the palladiums of 100% Americanism; the apostles of the Harding politics; the guardians of the Only True Christianity. They constitute the Chambers of Commerce, the Rotary Clubs, the Kiwanis Clubs, the Watch and Ward Societies, the Men and Religion Forward Movements, the Y.M.C.A. directorates, the Good Citizen Leagues. They are the advertisers who determine what is to go into the American newspapers and what is to stay out. They are the Leading Citizens, the speakers at banquets, the profiteers, the corruptors of politics, the supporters of evangelical Christianity, the peers of the realm. Babbitt is their archetype. He is no worse than most, and no better; he is the average American of the ruling minority in this hundred and forty-sixth year of the Republic. He is America incarnate, exuberant and exquisite. Study him well and you will know better what is the matter with the land we live in than you would know after plowing through a thousand such volumes as Walter Lippmann's *Public Opinion*. What Lippmann tried to do as a professor, laboriously and without imagination, Lewis has here done as an artist with a few vivid strokes. It is a very fine piece of work indeed.

Nor is all its merit in the central figure. It is not Babbitt that shines forth most gaudily, but the whole complex of Babbittry, Babbittism, Babbittismus. In brief, Babbitt is seen as no more than a single member of the society he lives in—a matter far more difficult to handle, obviously, than any mere character sketch. His every act is related to the phenomena of that society. It is not what he feels and aspires to that moves him primarily; it is what the folks about him will think of him. His politics is communal politics, mob politics, herd politics; his religion is a public rite wholly without subjective significance; his relations to his wife and his children are formalized and standardized; even his debaucheries are the orthodox debaucheries of a sound business man. The salient thing about him, in truth, is his complete lack of precisely the salient mark of every American of his class. What he feels and thinks is what it is currently proper to feel and think. Only once, during the two years that we have him under view, does he venture upon an idea that is even remotely original—and that time the heresy almost ruins him. The lesson, you may be sure, is not lost upon him. If he lives, he will not offend again. No thought will ever get a lodgment in his mind, even in the wildest, deliriums following bootleg gin, that will offer offense to the pruderies of Vergil Gunch, president of the Boosters' Club, or to those of old Mr. Eathorne, president of the First State Bank, or to those of the Rev. Dr. John Jennison Drew, pastor of the Chatham Road Presbyterian Church, or to those of Prof. Pumphrey, head of the Zenith

Business College, or even to those of Miss McGoun, the virtuous stenographer. He has been rolled through the mill. He emerges the very model and pattern of a forward-looking, right-thinking Americano.

As I say, this *Babbitt* gives me great delight. It is shrewdly devised; it is adeptly managed; it is well written. The details, as in *Main Street*, are extraordinarily vivid—the speech of Babbitt before the Zenith Real Estate Board, the meeting to consider ways and means of bulging the Chatham Road Sunday-school, the annual convention of the real-estate men, Babbitt's amour with the manicure-girl, the episode of Sir Gerald Doak, the warning visit when Babbitt is suspected of Liberalism, the New Thought meeting, the elopement of young Theodore Roosevelt Babbitt and Eunice Littlefield at the end. In all these scenes there is more than mere humor; there is searching truth. They reveal something; they mean something. I know of no American novel that more accurately presents the real America. It is a social document of a high order.

REBECCA WEST

Babbitt

*M*ain *Street* was a good book. One was as glad that it attained the incredibly tremendous triumph of being an American best-seller as one might be when a thoroughly nice girl wins the Calcutta Sweepstake. But on reading *Main Street* one did not in the least feel as if one were dancing round a bonfire. Heat and light and exhilaration were foreign to the hour. It was a sincere, competent, informative, even occasionally passionate piece of writing, but it had not that something extra and above the logical treatment of its subject—that "peacock's feather in the cap," as Yeats has called it— which makes the work of art. Moreover, it had not much in it of its author's own quality, and that was felt as a serious deprivation by those who were acquainted with Mr. Lewis and his literary past, by those who knew, for example, of the entertaining investigation into spiritualism he conducted on behalf of one of the American magazines. (During the course of this, swathing with seriousness a remarkable personal appearance which bears a strong resemblance to that of Mr. George Grossmith, but made more glorious with red hair, he sat down beside many mediums and asked chokingly for a message from his "dear friend, Mr. H. G. Wells, the English novelist, who recently passed over"; and usually got one.) But these deficiencies are rectified in *Babbitt*. It has that something extra, over and above, which makes the work of art, and it is signed in every line with the

From *Sinclair Lewis: A Collection of Critical Essays*, ed. Mark Schorer. © 1962 by Prentice Hall, Inc.

unique personality of the writer. It is saturated with America's vitality which makes one obey the rhythms of its dance music, which gives unlimited power over audiences to their actresses whether they be artistically dog-lazy like Ethel Levey, or negligible like Peggy O'Neill. And combined with this, Mr. Lewis has an individual gift of humour, a curiously sage devotion to craftsmanship, and a poetic passion for his own, new country.

To write satire is to perform a miracle. One must hate the world so much that one's hatred strikes sparks, but one must hate it only because it disappoints one's invincible love of it; one must write in denunciation of ugliness and put the thing down in unmistakable black and white, yet keep this, as all written things, within the sphere of beauty. But Mr. Lewis has been equal to these things. He writes of vulgar Zenith City and its vulgar children, yet never writes a vulgar line. He is merciless to George F. Babbitt, that standardised child of that standardised city, with his pad-cheeks and his puffy hands, his hypocrisy and his ignorance, his dishonesty and his timid sensualities; and he reveals him lovable and pitiable, a strayed soul disconsolate through frustrated desires for honour and beauty. He can flame into transports of exasperation with the religion of business and its paunchy priesthood—marvellous transports these are, for what we have here is the Celt getting angry with the Englishman. For Zenith City and Babbitt are amazingly English. They represent that section of America which seems the least affected by the Latin and Jewish and Celtic leavens; the resemblance of kinship is patent, even blatant. Oh, never star was lost here but it rose afar! Look West where whole new thousands are! In Zenith City what Leverhulme! And the Celt in the person of Mr. Lewis cannot bear it. Vindictively he reports their flat, endlessly repetitive, excessively and simultaneously ignorant and sophisticated conversation at dinner parties and in smoking-cars. He snatches out of the paper enraged parodies of the *Poemulations* they read instead of poetry—by T. Cholmondeley Frink, who was not only the author of *Poemulations*, which, syndicated daily in sixty-seven leading newspapers, gave him one of the largest audiences of any poet in the world, but also an optimistic lecturer and the creator of "Ads. that Add."

> I sat alone and groused and thunk, and scratched my head and
> sighed and wunk and groaned. There still are boobs, alack,
> who'd like the old time gin-mill back; that den, that makes a
> sage a loon, the vile and smelly old saloon! I'll never miss their
> poison booze, whilst I the bubbling spring can use, that leaves
> my head at merry morn as clear as any babe newborn!

He describes with deadly malice the proceedings at the lunch of the Zenith Boosters' Club. "The International Organisation of Boosters' Clubs has become a world-force for optimism, manly pleasantry, and good business." Its members all wore a button marked "Boosters—Pep!" At each place at the lunch-table, on the famous day when George F. Babbitt was elected Vice-President, was laid a present, a card printed in artistic red and black:

SERVICE AND BOOSTERISM.

Service finds its finest opportunity and development only in its broadest and deepest application and the consideration of its perpetual action upon reaction. I believe the highest type of Service, like the most progressive tenets of ethics, senses unceasingly and is motivated by active adherence and loyalty to that which is the essential principle of Boosterism—Good Citizenship in all its factors and aspects.

DAD PETERSEN.

Compliments of Dadbury Petersen Advertising Corp.
"Ads not Fads at Dads."

"The Boosters all read Mr. Petersen's aphorism and said they understood it perfectly."

Yet behind all this is a truth. There is something happening in among these hustling congregations of fat and absurd men. The present condition of George F. Babbitt may be discomfortable. Loathing at the smooth surface of his standardised life, destitute of interstices that might admit romance, may move him to vain and painful flights towards the promise of light; to his comical attempts to find spiritual comfort in the Chatham Street Presbyterian Church; to his efforts to make a synthetic substitute for love out of the kittenish contacts of Mrs. Tanis Judique. ("And shall I call you George? Don't you think it's awfully nice when two people have so much— what shall I say?—analysis that they can discard all these conventions and understand each other and become acquainted right away, like ships that pass in the night?") Little as he has, he yet possesses a promise. The value of that possession can be estimated by comparing Babbitt with his English analogue, Sir Gerald Doak, whom Mr. Lewis shows, touring the States in a state of panic because a title bought by the accumulations of industry in Nottingham brings on him the attentions of earnest hostesses who (misled by their conception of the British aristocracy) talk to him about polo and the galleries of Florence. Paunch for paunch these two sound business men seem much the same. But there is for Babbitt a certain advantage; or perhaps, in the transitional and blundering state of affairs revealed in this book, it should be called a certain opportunity. He moves in a setting so vast and so magnificent that surely it must ultimately dictate vastness and magnificence to the action it contains. There are in this volume a few pages, which must be counted among the masterpieces of satire; they profess to give a verbatim report of the speech delivered by Mr. George F. Babbitt at the Annual Dinner of The Zenith Real Estate Board. In it Mr. Lewis' exasperation rises to the pitch of genius. It dances on the chest of Babbitt's silly standardised self and his silly standardised world. There is one absurd passage, when Babbitt cries:

"With all modesty, I want to stand up here as a representative businessman and gently whisper, Here's our kind of folks! Here's the specifications of the standardised American Citizen! Here's the new generation of Americans: fellows with hair on their chests and smiles in their eyes and adding machines in their offices.... So! In my clumsy way I have tried to sketch the Real He-man, the fellow with Zep and Bang! And it's because Zenith has so large a proportion of such men, that it's the most stable, the greatest of our cities. New York also has its thousands of Real Folks, but New York is cursed with unnumbered foreigners. So are Chicago and San Francisco. Oh, we have a golden roster of cities—Detroit and Cleveland with their renowned factories. Cincinnati with its great machine-tool and soap products, Pittsburgh and Birmingham with their steel, Kansas City and Minneapolis and Omaha that open their bountiful gates on the bosom of the ocean-like wheatlands, and countless other magnificent sister-cities, for by the last census, there were no less than sixty-eight glorious American burgs with a population of over one hundred thousand! And all these cities stand together for power and purity, and against foreign ideas and communism. Atlanta with Hartford, Rochester with Denver, Milwaukee with Indianapolis, Los Angeles with Scranton, Portland, Maine, with Portland, Oregon. A good live-wire from Baltimore, or Seattle or Duluth is the twin brother of every like fellow booster from Buffalo or Akron, Fort Worth or Oskaloosa!"

It is a bonehead Walt Whitman speaking. Stuffed like a Christmas goose as Babbitt is, with silly films, silly newspapers, silly talk, silly oratory, there has yet struck him the majestic creativeness of his own country, its miraculous power to bear and nourish without end countless multitudes of men and women. He is so silly, so ill-educated (though as he says, "the State University is my own Alma Mater, and I am proud to be known as an alumni") that he prefers to think of it bearing and nourishing countless multitudes of featureless standardised Regular Guys. But there is in these people a vitality so intense that it must eventually bolt with them and land them willy-nilly into the sphere of intelligence; and this immense commercial machine will become the instrument of their aspiration.

Before he followed his wife, Babbitt stood at the westernmost window of their room. This residential settlement, Floral Heights, was on a rise; and though the centre of the city was three miles away—Zenith had between three and four hundred thousand inhabitants now—he could see the top of the Second National Tower, an Indiana limestone building of thirty-five storeys.

Its shining wall rose against April sky to a simple cornice like a streak of white fire. Integrity was in the tower, and decision. It bore its strength lightly as a tall soldier. As Babbitt stared, the nervousness was soothed from his face, his slack chin lifted in reverence. All he articulated was, "That's one lovely sight!" but he was inspired by the rhythm of the city; his love of it renewed. He beheld the tower as a temple-spire of the religion of business, a faith passionate, exalted, surpassing common men; and as he clumped down to breakfast he whistled the ballad, "Oh, by gee, by gosh, by jingo," as though it were a hymn melancholy and noble.

SHERWOOD ANDERSON

Sinclair Lewis

Of the four American writers concerning whose handling of our speech I have had the temerity to express my own feeling there is left Mr. Sinclair Lewis.

The texture of the prose written by Mr. Lewis gives me but faint joy and I cannot escape the conviction that for some reason Lewis has himself found but little joy, either in life among us or in his own effort to channel his reactions to our life into prose. There can be no doubt that this man, with his sharp journalistic nose for news of the outer surface of our lives, has found out a lot of things about us and the way we live in our towns and cities, but I am very sure that in the life of every man, woman and child in the country there are forces at work that seem to have escaped the notice of Mr. Lewis. Mr. Ring Lardner has seen them and in his writing there is sometimes real laughter, but one has the feeling that Lewis never laughs at all, that he is in an odd way too serious about something to laugh.

For after all, even in Gopher Prairie or in Indianapolis, Indiana, boys go swimming in the creeks on summer afternoons, shadows play at evening on factory walls, old men dig angleworms and go fishing together, love comes to at least a few men and women, and everything else failing, the baseball club comes from a neighboring town and Tom Robinson gets a home run. That's something. There is an outlook on life across which even

From *Sinclair Lewis: A Collection of Critical Essays*, ed. Mark Schorer. © 1962 by Prentice Hall, Inc.

the cry of a child, choked to death by its own mother, would be something. Life in our American towns and cities is barren enough and there are enough people saying that with the growth of industrialism it has become continually more and more ugly, but Mr. Paul Rosenfeld and Mr. Ring Lardner apparently do not find it altogether barren and ugly. For them and for a growing number of men and women in America there is something like a dawn that Mr. Lewis has apparently sensed but little, for there is so little sense of it in the texture of his prose. Reading Mr. Sinclair Lewis, one comes inevitably to the conclusion that here is a man writing who, wanting passionately to love the life about him, cannot bring himself to do so, and who, wanting perhaps to see beauty descend upon our lives like a rainstorm, has become blind to the minor beauties our lives hold.

And is it not just this sense of dreary spiritual death in the man's work that is making it so widely read? To one who is himself afraid to live there is, I am sure, a kind of joy in seeing other men as dead. In my own feeling for the man from whose pen has come all of this prose over which there are so few lights and shades, I have come at last to sense, most of all, the man fighting terrifically and ineffectually for a thing about which he really does care. There is a kind of fighter living inside Mr. Sinclair Lewis and there is, even in this dull, unlighted prose of his, a kind of dawn coming. In the dreary ocean of this prose, islands begin to appear. In *Babbitt* there are moments when the people of whom he writes, with such amazing attention to the outer details of lives, begin to think and feel a little, and with the coming of life into his people a kind of nervous, hurried beauty and life flits, like a lantern carried by a night watchman past the window of a factory as one stands waiting and watching in a grim street on a night of December.

STEPHEN S. CONROY

Sinclair Lewis's Sociological Imagination

Sinclair Lewis was a novelist blessed with what C. Wright Mills called "the sociological imagination," the capacity to see and be interested in the overriding dramatic quality of "the interplay of man and society, of biography and history, of self and world."[1] Lewis was often accused of being a kind of social scientist, although usually the similarity noted was in investigative and preparatory techniques and not in quality of mind. Mark Schorer for example pointed out that "with Lewis, the subject, the social section always came first; systematic research, sometimes conducted by research assistants and carrying Lewis himself into 'the field' like any cultural anthropologist, followed; the story came last, devised to carry home and usually limping under the burden of data."[2] And Lewis too recognized the assumptions which underlay most of his work; he certainly was aware that his habits of mind and method of composition resembled the habits and practices of the social scientist. Most writers, he tells us, when asked what form the first idea of a story takes, will reply that they think first of a plot, of a person, or even of a setting. But speaking of his own practice Lewis says, "Actually, these three are from the beginning mixed in your minds you want to do a story about a person who, as he becomes real to you, dwells in a definite house, street, city, class of society."[3] It is, of course, this view of the individual imbedded in a matrix of neighborhood, city, and class which constitutes the basis of the sociological imagination.

From *American Literature* 42, Issue 3 (November 1970). © 1970 by Duke University Press.

The power that this matrix has over the behavior of the individual is enormous. The universal recognition of this fact leads many to conclude that the human individual is completely bound up and hemmed in by his culture. Yet somehow the human remains intractably human and stubbornly individualistic. He believes that he has free will and the acts on that faith; he often rebels, questions, and struggles against any confining force. The individual who does this is capable of becoming, in his own eyes at least, a worthy opponent of the collective will of society. The "interplay" Mills speaks of then becomes a kind of combat, a drama whose resolution is not always tragic, even though the antagonists are grossly unequal. The observer with the sociological imagination is one who is aware that this drama is being played out around him and focuses on it. He may be either a social scientist or an artist; the important factor is his view of life, not his professional preoccupations. Without question, Sinclair Lewis's imaginative frame of reference was sociological.

Given the nature of the struggle occurring, the problem for Sinclair Lewis, as for any novelist of a similar bent, is to determine just what responses or alternative modes of behavior are available to the protagonist vis-à-vis his culture. It is to Lewis's credit that he anticipated the formulations of David Riesman and even went beyond them in at least one instance. Riesman too, of course, possesses the sociological imagination, with perhaps a more legitimate claim to it than Lewis. In *The Lonely Crowd* and other works Riesman theorized about the responses open to the individual and concluded that there were only three: adjustment, anomie, and autonomy. Adjustment means conformity to the universals of the culture and an acceptance of the narrow range of choice left to the individual. Anomie in an individual, on the other hand, is virtually synonymous with maladjustment. A characteristic of the anomic is that he is never able to conform or feel comfortable in the roles: assigned to him by society since he rejects its traditional norms and values. The third possibility is autonomy. The autonomous person may or may not conform. He makes choices; he lives up to the culture's norms when it is advantageous for him to do so, and he transcends them when there are reasons to do so.[4] Lewis depicts two kinds of autonomy, positive and negative. He realized that the man indifferent to the demands of his culture could use his freedom for either good or evil.

The major works of Sinclair Lewis's greatest decade may be shown to be the working out in dramatic form of these sociological insights. *Main Street* and *Babbitt* both show the sometimes painful process of adjustment. *Arrowsmith*, on the other hand, is concerned with a protagonist who cannot adjust, one who becomes ever more alienated as his life unfolds. Finally,

Elmer Gantry and *Dodsworth* concern men who are autonomous in two different ways.

Carol Kennicott, the heroine of *Main Street*, is usually characterized as a brave young bride who struggles pridefully against the spiteful parochialism of a prairie village, but George F. Babbitt is generally thought of as a near-villain of urbanized conformity. Usually overlooked is their similarity of outlook and aspiration, and the parallelism of their fates. They are both unhappy and restless in the society in which they find themselves; they both rebel ineffectually, and they both finally become largely adjusted to their surroundings. There are differences, of course, but they are often overemphasized at the expense of more important similarities.

Carol goes through a definite three-stage process of rebellion, withdrawal from and reconciliation to Gopher Prairie. Her rebellion begins with her first tour of Main Street during which she is repelled by its ugly drabness. She also overreacts to the general blankness of the town society and to the dullness of her new companions. She then overcompensates with almost frenzied activity, gives silly but lively parties, and takes up and drops many useless projects. The village misunderstands her vitality and rebuffs her efforts. Carol feels, appropriately enough, that the townsfolk have rejected her, and she also suspects that they are scoffing at her. This reaction of the town has a double-edged effect on Carol. In one way it deepens her rebellion and causes her to involve herself in a situation even further outside the town's standard of acceptable behavior; it causes her flirtation with an ardent young apprentice tailor, which could have led to public scandal and disgrace. That it does not is due, paradoxically enough, to the town itself, for she rejects the young man's advances largely because she has grown to fear Gopher Prairie. She has made the first step in the process of adjustment when she cuts off a personal relationship for social reasons. Even if her action is largely motivated by terror, it constitutes a recognition on her part (and on Lewis's) of the power of the society to control behavior.

When rebellion within the confines of Gopher Prairie proves to be either impossible or too costly, Carol takes a step toward withdrawal. Her removal to Washington, D.C., like her earlier rebellion, is paradoxically but a step in her ultimate adjustment. Washington's sophistication and refinement prove not to be enough to replace the loss of family and status. She spends a good deal of time planning someday to take her son back to the open fields and friendly barns around Gopher Prairie. Also, in Washington she learns that there are Main Streets everywhere, and as Lewis tells us, in comparison to some Gopher Prairie's is a model of beauty and intelligence. In addition she begins to see that there is a thick streak of Main Street in Washington and doubtlessly in other large cities as well, a truism which

George Babbitt is soon to learn in Zenith. Thus is the way paved for a reconciliation with her village; her sojourn in Washington has enabled her to come to terms with Gopher Prairie. "At last," she rejoiced, "I've come to a fairer attitude toward the town. I can love it now." Her view becomes more than fair, even hazily romantic. "She again saw Gopher Prairie as her home, waiting for her in the sunset, rimmed round with splendor...."[5]

At the end of *Main Street* Carol Kennicott is at home in Gopher Prairie in every sense of the word. She has not been beaten into submission; she has decided to adjust. Her return home is the result of three factors: her desire for her son to grow up in what she presumes to be the healthy environment of the prairie village, her love for her husband, and her newfound love for the town itself. Near the conclusion of the novel Carol voluntarily gets into the back seat of an automobile with a woman friend in order to let their "menfolk" sit together in the front. This symbolic act shows her to be, all unaware, finally a true citizen of Gopher Prairie. Originally Carol had too strongly insisted on her individuality against the pressure of her culture. She engaged in a battle which she could not win on her own terms; she did not have either the personal force or the social backing to change the ways of the town significantly. She either had to continue fighting and paying the terrible personal costs involved, or she had to adjust. Adjustment of course spells defeat for her aspirations, but it is a peculiar kind of defeat, almost without sting. When Carol adjusts she is comfortable in her adjustment; only occasional, and mild, twinges remain, and only for a time.

Babbitt's struggle is very little different from Carol Kennicott's. He too squirms uneasily under the pressure of his society, rebels against it, and finally returns meekly to conformity to it. There is one important difference between Carol Kennicott and George F. Babbitt; Carol comes as an outsider into Gopher Prairie, but Babbitt is a longtime citizen of Zenith. Carol reacts to the village as if it were an icy pool she had just been thrown into; her immediate and almost overwhelming desire is to get out. Babbitt, on the other hand, is immersed in his surroundings as in a warm bath. As Edith Wharton observed, "Babbitt is in and of Zenith up to his chin and over."[6] Only gradually does he come to realize that something is wrong with his society and with his position in it.

The emphasis in the beginning of the novel is on Babbitt as conformist, although he has already become aware of some disturbing impulses. He conforms outwardly but he is no longer completely adjusted; he has vague dissatisfactions and is full of veiled rebellions and escapist daydreams. What finally sets Babbitt loose, what causes such a conformist to go so far astray, are the shocking events surrounding Paul Riesling's attempted murder of his wife, his trial and imprisonment. After the sentencing, "Babbitt returned to his office to realize that he faced a world which, without Paul, was meaningless."[7] And so his rebellion begins.

When a conformist becomes rebellious, when he is, as Lewis says of Babbitt, "determined to go astray," what can he do? He can stray sexually, or at least try to; Babbitt's attempts to seduce first a neighbor's coquettish wife and then a tough young manicurist meet with little success. These episodes are the somewhat more shabby equivalent of Carol Kennicott's flirtation with a tailor's apprentice, and are no more meaningful. There is also with Babbitt, as there was with Carol, a compulsion to make the rebellion known. Babbitt is impelled to make a public display of his disenchantment with Zenith, and his display takes two forms. The first part of his rebellion consists of an entanglement with the bohemian element of the city, and continues with an adulterous affair with one of its leaders, Tanis Judique. The second part of his rebellion is political rather than sexual or social. He publicly avows some of the positions of the liberal minority, defends "radicals," and refuses to join an organization devoted to the repression of dissent. Although the first part of his rebellion is more colorful, the second part proves more dangerous to him.

Carol Kennicott had skirted the edge of adultery, but was saved by her feelings for her husband, her fear of the town, and her own fastidiousness. George F. Babbitt at first seems to have none of these problems; he engages in open adultery without bringing the wrath of society down on him, perhaps only an illustration of the double standard, but perhaps also one slight demonstration of the somewhat greater sophistication of Zenith compared to Gopher Prairie. Babbitt's tawdry affair and his infatuation with the bohemian fringe are frowned upon by society, but they invoke no very strong sanction. Babbitt increasingly finds his relationship with Tanis Judique cloying, and her friends less and less tolerable. In the last analysis, ironic as it may sound, Babbitt breaks away from Tanis and "the bunch" because of his sense of fastidiousness; he too has in some small measure that element so outstanding in the makeup of Carol Kennicott.

Carol never really feels the full weight of her society's displeasure; Babbitt, however, receives penalties ranging from loss of business through threats of ostracism and even violence. To the Good Citizen's League he almost becomes one of that undesirable element, parlor socialists. He is informed exactly what the league has in store for him unless he changes his activities: "One of the best ways it can put the kibosh on cranks is to apply this social boycott business to folks big enough so you can't reach them otherwise. Then if that don't work, the G.C.L. can finally send a little delegation around to inform folks that get too flip that they got to conform to decent standards and quit shooting off their mouths so free."[8] The threat involved in the last part of the statement is not lost on Babbitt; he becomes slightly paranoic and begins to feel that he is being spied upon.

Babbitt is a rather stubborn man, so that fearful as he is, he will not give in to these pressures. It would have been interesting to see how far society would have moved against him, and at what point he would have broken down. But Lewis is not yet willing to let the conflict between an individual and his culture work itself out. With perfect timing, Myra Babbitt is rushed off to the hospital for an emergency appendectomy. Her surgery and extended recovery give Babbitt and his clan a pretext for patching up their squabble. With his wife's illness, the hostility toward Babbitt seems to disappear. He is even given another chance to join the Good Citizen's League, and "within two weeks no one in the League was more violent regarding the wickedness of Seneca Doane, the crimes of labor unions, the perils of immigration, and the delights of gold, morality, and bank accounts than was George F. Babbitt."9

Thus is Babbitt's conformist nature splendidly reestablished; once again he sinks into his culture "up to his chin and over." Yet, once again, like Carol Kennicott, he is not completely submerged. He is the adjusted man, but there is in him as in Carol a residue of dissatisfaction. In both cases it is displaced onto the next generation. Carol looks upon her daughter as the one who will win the struggle with the village culture, and Babbitt defends his son's life plan even though it is not very promising. Babbitt urges him to have courage and to do what he wishes to do with his life. To Babbitt as to Carol children represent the hope for a brighter future. This hope is, of course, the culturally approved way in which a defeated rebel may find solace. Lewis still saw this deferred and displaced gratification as the best solution to the problem facing the individualist in a culture demanding conformity. The bohemian response he had no taste for, and he still seems largely unaware of the possibility of real autonomy. There is in *Babbitt* no character with the requisite intelligence and force to make the autonomous response. All that is left is conformity, adjustment, and a vague hope for a freer future.

In *Arrowsmith* the case is somewhat different. The individual's struggle with the demands of his culture is dramatized as the struggle between intensely individualistic dedication to scientific research and increasing tempting offers of worldly success. Martin Arrowsmith receives offers of success or potential success of a material sort often enough in his career. When he decides to leave Wheatsylvania, he is reminded by his father-in-law of the great sums he could soon be making, is offered a partnership in the village drugstore, and is tempted by certain political office. In Nautilus, Iowa, where he is a public health physician, a banker offers to finance him in setting up a private practice, and in the Rouncefield Clinic in Chicago he is constantly told that soon he will be made a partner and be eligible for a share of rather substantial profits. Martin, however, is not to he turned away forever from his chosen goal of medical research. He fights his way on to the prestigious McGurk Institute in New York, but is soon disillusioned to find as much importance given there to appearances, income, and status as in Wheatsylvania. He has climbed to the pinnacle and has found it too corrupted by America's materialistic standards. There is nowhere else for him to go within the system, and so in final despair he drops out of society altogether to become a kind of scientific monk cloistered in a Vermont farm.

The alienated or maladjusted man refuses to accept his culture, often withdraws from it, and tends to isolate himself within an impossible dreamworld. Isolation is a solution which cannot work, by virtue of the very lack of any meaningful interaction with an ongoing society. Sheldon Grebstein, however, maintains that "what Lewis suggested by Arrowsmith's withdrawal from civilization was simply a refusal by the individual to be bound by conventional social codes, mores, or patterns of behavior," and he goes on to observe that this is an expression of Lewis's fundamental optimism, for it proves that "happiness can be found in America."[10] Only in a very restricted sense is Grebstein correct. If America is defined solely as a geographic entity, then *Arrowsmith* does prove that happiness can be found there, for the monastic cabin to which Martin ultimately retreats is located within the boundaries of the United States. But if America is defined in the larger sense of a system of "conventional social codes, mores, or patterns of behavior," then Arrowsmith does not find happiness there.

The ending of *Arrowsmith* leaves much to be desired. It shows that Lewis continued to avoid a logical working out of real social conflict. In earlier works Lewis could somehow modulate the issues so that a resolution could seem to be achieved in terms of something as simple as the relationship between a man and a woman. Thus both Carol Kennicott and George F. Babbitt are shown to be in conflict with their respective spouses as well as with the surrounding culture, and the individual–culture struggle is resolved by solving the marital struggle. In *Arrowsmith*, however, Lewis is pushed to some unlikely plot devices. He finds it necessary to kill off the appealing Leora Arrowsmith, for Martin could not have left her and maintained the reader's sympathy, and with her his hegira into the woods would be either pointless or impossible. But Joyce, his wealthy second wife, was a good representative of the society from which he felt impelled to withdraw, and therefore she could be left behind without being cruelly abandoned.

In this novel Lewis shows the conflict between the individual American and the demands of his culture becoming more serious, and the solution for the individual becoming more difficult. In *Main Street* and *Babbitt* he says that the culture is a poor one but that it can be lived in, and that the best, perhaps the only, solution to the struggle is for the individual to surrender himself to society's norms. But this is not the solution offered in *Arrowsmith*. Martin's withdrawal from society, no matter how romantic it seems to be on the surface, is an act of despair. Unlike Carol Kennicott and George Babbitt, both of whom look to their children's future for justification, Martin Arrowsmith feels nothing but dismay when contemplating his son's future and their relationship. Lewis tells us that "Martin was afraid of him, because he saw that this minuscule aristocrat, this child born to the self-approval of riches, would some day condescend to him."[11]

No matter how it is viewed, Martin Arrowsmith's solution to the culture–individual conflict is an gnomic one. He gives up family, wealth, status, and almost all human contact because of his devotion to medical research. In this particular instance, since both Martin and his alter ego, Terry Wickett, have highly marketable skills, there is a possibility that they can survive on a few hours a day devoted to economically productive work, freeing the rest of their time for pure research. But their solution is not one that can be used as a model by others in a similar predicament. For most people this sort of total withdrawal from society is not possible, except perhaps at the price of sanity. Even the conformist solution of a Babbitt is preferable to that. Perhaps Sinclair Lewis realized this, for in his next two books he examined another alternative—autonomy.

If a man is not adjusted to his culture there seem to be only two possibilities open to him. He can alienate himself completely from the culture—the solution Martin Arrowsmith tries—or he can become autonomous. The autonomous man is not withdrawn; he is detached. He separates himself emotionally but not cognitively from the culture, nor does he withdraw physically from it. Autonomy is the solution Elmer Gantry finds, for his aberrant behavior goes far beyond mere nonconformity. Introducing him, Lewis says, "Elmer assumed that he was the center of the universe, and that the rest of the system was valuable only as it afforded him help and pleasure."[12] No other Lewis protagonist has Elmer's colossal sense of self-importance. A man who can look detachedly at his culture and see it for what it is must be a person of much self-containment. Gantry's ego is such that his image of himself surpasses mere self-containment; it is so inflated that he views the culture as something less than, it is in reality.

Throughout the novel Lewis emphasizes Gantry's lack of commitment to the realities of his culture by employing theatrical allusions. His pulpit appearances are almost always described as if he were on stage. "As an actor enjoyed greasepaint ... so Elmer had the affection of familiarity for ... the drama of coming from the mysteries backstage, so unknown and fascinating to the audience, to the limelight of the waiting congregation."[13] The conceit is carried out in great detail: actor, greasepaint, drama, backstage, audience, limelight. He gloats later, "Never had he known such sincerity of histrionic instinct."[14] Moreover, Lewis does not limit the stage analogies to a description of Elmer Gantry at the altar. He points out, for instance, that Gantry is careful of his appearance by saying, "He dressed as calculating as an actor."[15] And finally, not to belabor the point, Elmer on first meeting his millionaire benefactor, T. J. Riggs, cautions himself to be careful because, "He's onto me."[16] Unless Elmer Gantry is not what he tries to appear to be, unless he is acting, there is no reason for him to fear that someone will get "onto" him.

Since he is such an actor, and because he is so blithely evil, Elmer Gantry poses problems both for the critic and for the social scientist who has equated the autonomous man with the hero. Elmer Gantry is obviously autonomous; he transcends the norms for the adjusted with a vengeance, although in the wrong direction. And he is surely no hero; the truth is that he is a villain—an evil autonomous man. This is a possibility Riesman and others do not explore to any great extent, the possibility that there can be, as it were, both negative and positive autonomy. Elmer Gantry is both evil and autonomous, but his autonomy is negatively charged, being both destructive and morally corrupt. If Lewis saw Gantry in this light, as no doubt he did, it is no wonder that he became more reconciled to "adjustment" later in his career. Lewis has been criticized for abandoning his satirical attacks and becoming an apologist for American culture as he grew older. In part he did so, and his change of heart or manner is understandable as a revulsion against the immoral antisocietal type represented by Gantry.

But Sinclair Lewis had not as yet exhausted the list of possible reactions of the individual to his culture. There is the possibility of another sort of autonomous man. In his next work, *Dodsworth*, Lewis portrays a figure whose autonomy is positive rather than negative. Sam Dodsworth, when first we see him, is a man living in a world of things as they are and not as they ought to be. Lewis makes of him a man who grows: a man who begins as a conformist, gradually gains perspective, and even with this new insight does not reject his culture. In the beginning he is what sociologists would call an adjusted man; he is comfortable in his culture. As he says of himself, "Why, I never thought much about America as a whole. Sort of taken it for granted—."[17] This was his response the first time his American assumptions were challenged in Europe. Much later he is rather amused at his earlier naiveté, or rather, his earlier unthinking acceptance of all things American. He tries to recapture what it was that he *had* believed and says, "I suppose I felt that the entire known world revolved around the General Offices of the Revelation Motor

Company, Constitution Avenue, Zenith."[18] From the man who takes things for granted to the man who analyzes is certainly a great step; for Sam Dodsworth the step is a change based on the painful process of hard thought.

Dodsworth is an intelligent man, but he has not been trained in analytic thought; on the contrary, he has been trained out of it. The welter of his new experiences in Europe demanded cataloging, and the most effective way of doing this was by comparing these new experiences to familiar ones from home. It was not an easy process for him because it demanded that he think "almost impersonally," and "it was a new occupation for him, and he was a little confused."[19] But once this analysis begins it continues almost of its own volition. As it continues it is rewarding but uncomfortable; as Lewis says, "All thinking about matters less immediate than food, sex, business, and the security of one's children is a disease and Sam was catching it."[20] What he is catching will not make him happy, Lewis suggests, for the more one is aware of, the more there is to be hurt and puzzled by. Dodsworth finds his awakening not particularly pleasurable. Thinking about impersonal things like cultural differences leads to pondering for extended periods about them: "thus brooding hour-long, ... thus slowly and painfully perceiving a world vaster than he had known."[21] When an intelligent man begins to think, to ponder, to brood about his society and its relationship to other societies in the world, he begins to detach himself intellectually from his own culture. No matter how much of a conformist he is in the beginning, no matter how well adjusted, he most certainly will gain a certain amount of autonomy. He has gained aesthetic distance from his society; he is no longer immersed in it, and he no longer accepts its ways as given. He may or may not decide to obey any particular norm, for he now has freedom of choice; in a word, he is autonomous.

One sign of Dodsworth's autonomy is the critical attitude he takes toward the ideas of his old friends from Zenith. He can no longer completely accept their opinions on economics and politics, although he is not yet completely detached either. His objectivity at such a time indirectly reveals one way in which Lewis structured the novel. Lewis has Dodsworth's gradual awakening to the nature of his culture parallel in many ways his gradual awakening to the true nature of his wife. The paths of Dodsworth's awakening regarding the nature of his wife and of his culture are parallel but do not lead to the same conclusion, for Dodsworth ultimately rejects his wife but he does not reject his culture. Interestingly enough, when he returns to America he will return with a new wife, for although he has rejected a wife he has not rejected the institution of marriage, nor the other institutions of American culture. But it seems clear that he will treat Edith differently from the way he treated Bran, just as he most surely will have a new outlook on his society.

In the last scene in the novel Dodsworth and his soon-to-be wife share an experience which captures in miniature much of what the novel is about: "They were dining at the Ritz in Paris, Edith and Sam, feeling superior to its pretentiousness, because that evening they had determined to return to America, when his divorce should be complete, and to experiment with caravans. They were gay, well dined and well content."[22] The Ritz is symbolic here of European civilization with all its rococo gaudiness as compared to the plain honesty of American civilization, and as Americans they feel superior to Europeans, especially now that they have learned all they can from them. And the word used to describe their decision to return is "determined," which denotes here a conscious and fairly difficult act of the will, for now they have lost their innocence as regards their culture; they will see its flaws as well as its good points. And one of the good points is that in the United States Sam will find useful, craftsmanlike work in experimenting with camping trailers, for America is a place, as they see it, of experimentation and new beginnings.

Of all Lewis's novels of the 1920's, *Dodsworth* is the one in which his hero finds the most satisfactory answer to the demands of his culture. Samuel Dodsworth, a good man, will return to the arms of his culture, but he will be autonomous in it. He will not sink into conformity as did Carol Kennicott and George F. Babbitt; he will not indulge in romantic rejection of it as did Martin Arrowsmith; and he will certainly not cynically "use" his culture as did Elmer Gantry. Samuel Dodsworth will be as autonomous as Gantry, but his autonomy will be a positive one, for he will add to his culture and try to change it for the better. This is also Lewis's most optimistic novel of the twenties, for it shows him in good measure reconciled to his culture. He does not picture forced adjustment to desperate escape from, or cynical misuse of the culture. American civilization can be lived in, Lewis at last affirms, if only one knows how.

With *Dodsworth* Sinclair Lewis reached the end of his greatest period. He had by this time used up all the possible responses an individual could make to his culture. He had used conformity twice, anomie once, and autonomy twice, or rather positive autonomy once and negative autonomy once. And so Lewis found himself in a dilemma perhaps without being aware of it. His imagination still continued to present life to him in terms of man versus culture, but he had exhausted the possibilities of fresh action for the individual. He was condemned by the sociological quality of his imagination to repeat himself as an artist.

Lewis tried two or three ways out of the dilemma he found himself in. At least once in his later career he forced his imagination out of its sociological mold, and wrote a historical romance, *The God Seeker*, but it was a flat failure. He also tried what might be called reverse polarity. In *The Prodigal Parents* he made the society good and the individual bad; much more so here than in *Babbitt* he celebrates the conformist as hero. But the novel is an incredibly poor one; Granville Hicks with justice entitled his review of it, "Sinclair Lewis' Stinkbomb."[23] Similarly, in *It Can't Happen Here* Lewis leaped a few years into the future and altered American society so far in the direction of fascism that behavior which would now be conformist then becomes rebellious. *It Can't Happen Here* is one of the best of the later novels, but by its very nature it was a one-time performance. It pointed no new way out of Lewis's artistic dilemma.

Sinclair Lewis was, by the limitations of his sociological imagination, forced into repetition. *Cass Timberlane* is much like a middle-aged *Main Street*; *Gideon Planish* is a pale imitation of *Elmer Gantry*; *World So Wide* is an even paler copy of *Dodsworth*; and *Work of Art* substitutes an obsession with hotelkeeping for *Arrowsmith*'s picture of dedication to science. There are other novels, some of which contain echoes of more than one of Lewis's greater works, but *every* later book is repetitive in some fashion or other. The sociological imagination of Sinclair Lewis, grasping the cultural setting of American life, seeing the drama inherent in the struggle of an individual with his society, and working out in dramatic fashion the possibilities for individual response which David Riesman would later give names to, is responsible in no small part for the very real worth of the products of Lewis's great decade. But on the other hand, the limited nature of this sort of imagination is also responsible for the sense of *déjà vu* one cannot escape while reading Lewis's later novels; the reader has indeed been there before.

NOTES

1. *The Sociological Imagination* (New York, 1959), p. 4.

2. "Sinclair Lewis and the Method of Half-truths" in *Sinclair Lewis: A Collection of Critical Essays*, ed. Mark Schorer (Englewood Cliffs, N.J., 1962), pp. 48–49.

3. Harry E. Maule and Melville H. Cane, eds., *The Man From Main Street: Selected Essays and Other Writings, 1904–1950* (New York, 1953), p. 187.

4. David Riesman, with Nathan Glazer and Reuel Denney, *The Lonely Crowd* (Garden City, N.Y., 1955), pp. 278–280.

5. Sinclair Lewis, *Main Street* (New York, 1920), pp. 442–443.

6. Mark Schorer, *Sinclair Lewis: An American Life* (New York, 1961), p. 346.

7. Sinclair Lewis, *Babbitt* (New York, 1922), p. 269.

8. Ibid., p. 346.

9. Ibid., p. 390.

10. "Sinclair Lewis: American Social Critic" (doctoral dissertation, Michigan State University, 1954), p. 147.

11. Sinclair Lewis, *Arrowsmith* (New York, .1925), p. 433.

12. Sinclair Lewis, *Elmer Gantry* (New York, 1927), p. 7.

13. Ibid., p. 258.

14. Ibid., p, 272.
15. Ibid., p. 318.
16. Ibid., p. 315.
17. Sinclair Lewis, *Dodsworth* (New York, 1929), p. 43.
18. Ibid., p. 126.
19. Ibid., p. 92.
20. Ibid., p. 191.
21. Ibid., p. 326.
22. Ibid., p. 376.
23. *New Masses*, XXVI (Jan. 25, 1938), 19.

DICK WAGENAAR

The Knight and the Pioneer: Europe and America and the Fiction of Sinclair Lewis

If it is true, as E. M. Forster noted, that Sinclair Lewis managed to "lodge a piece of a continent in our imagination," it would be no less true to observe that in a sense this achievement required constant appeals to his image of another continent.[1] That continent, of course, was "Yurrup," or, more conventionally, Europe. Though ranged against the entire *oeuvre* few of the novels address the European question directly, all reflect the influence of what Lewis believed Europe to be and to mean. Certainly it is not without significance that the bulk of events in both his very first book, *Our Mr. Wrenn* (1914),[2] and his very last book, *World So Wide* (1951), should occur in a European setting, a setting not sketched in as accidental background but treated in such a way as to constitute an important strain in the novels' thematic structure. Moreover, that he should have turned at the end of his glorious decade,[3] presumably secure in the feeling that he was at the height of his powers—having with *Main Street* (1920), *Babbitt* (1922), *Arrowsmith* (1925), and *Elmer Gantry* (1927) persuaded his critics that his apprenticeship had made way for a certain mastery and not yet suspecting that this mastery would soon disintegrate—to a direct confrontation with Europe in *Dodsworth* (1929) testifies to a compelling interest in the subject.

Such a preoccupation is not uncharacteristic of American thought. One of our most persistent literary impulses has been the attempt to define

From *American Literature* 50, Issue 2 (May 1978). © 1978 by Duke University Press.

America by contrasting it with Europe. Especially when economic and military power began to give substance to our mystique of inhabiting some sort of "promised land," both pride in our material accomplishments and a certain anxiety about our possible spiritual shortcomings conspired to convince us of having an identity and a destiny that were unique, special in a way that demanded formulation in a vision which would somehow fix the essence of who, as a people, we were and what, as a nation, we could do, "We have listened too long to the courtly muses of Europe," said Emerson to his Harvard audience in 1837.[4] It was not the first time such sentiments had been expressed, and it would not be the last. But despite the air of defiance we have been exhorted to assume—the various characterizations of Europe as unsanitary or depraved by Lewis's various Boosters and Rotarians demonstrate how easily Emerson's lofty conception degenerated when it penetrated the popular mind—Europe has continued to constitute something of a starting point, a culture which when placed in juxtaposition to our own was presumed to give us a more accurate picture of ourselves.

When the Germans—Goethe, Nietzsche, Mann—headed south toward Italy, and the French—Flaubert, Rimbaud, Gide—embarked for North Africa, they rarely did so impelled by the earnest reasons with which literary nineteenth and early twentieth century Americans sailed for Europe. They certainly did not leave with the intention of discovering their national identity. If Nietzsche found sun and clear air in the Italian Alps, and Gide found compliant boys in the Algerian desert, and Rimbaud a profitable gun-running trade in the interior of Abyssinia, Americans bound for Europe were supposed to find, in the end, America. Needless to say, personal motivations often inspired the excursion, but, generally, "doing the continent" has been envisioned as one step in a cultural education whose underlying purpose was to reject Europe and to affirm America with renewed enthusiasm. Not always did the injunction prove itself impervious to Europe's charms. The number of those who never returned is not small. Reflecting the familiar pattern of his own novels—the rebellious hero returning to the fold—Lewis, unlike Henry James, Edith Wharton, or T. S. Eliot, did return, though not without those grave reservations of which his books might be said to form the record.

For Lewis, this cultural education began in Sauk Centre, Minnesota, a spot on the map likely to have remained beyond the reach of Europe's alluring power had his father's house not contained a certain number of books, and books of a certain kind. Reading Scott, Kipling, Hugo, Tennyson, he dreamed of a Europe where brave knights and beautiful ladies lived lives of chivalric propriety and heroic adventure against a background of enchanted forests and picturesque castles.[5] This romantic view of Europe not even the commonplace Europe he personally experienced later was able to deflate, no matter how much he might protest with Olivia Lomond of *World So Wide* that he recognized its illusory character:

> 'For a while I fell into an illusion—it doubtless came from overmuch reading of medieval chronicles and ballads, but still, it was childish and inexcusable—an illusion that a man ought to be obviously splendid: the knight crusader, daring and poetic, the Duke of Urbino, the battle-breaker, the patron of poets and artists; powerful, cloaked in brocade, belted with a great sword, surrounded by medieval color and all the respect of a medieval court.'[6]

Olivia's description of what sort of man she has dreamed about reflects much of what sort of Europe Lewis dreamed about. And, like Olivia, he suffered the constant tension between an intellectual awareness of fact and an emotional need for fancy. He could not help accepting the fact of Europe's reality falling far short of the dreams he had entertained about it, but emotionally the illusion was necessary. Since those reveries of grace and grandeur, daring and dashing, elegance and refinement, had afforded him his only joy in that lonely growing up in that dreary Minnesota town, he must have felt unable to discard them without both committing some essential betrayal of his fondest childhood hopes and forever forestalling himself from finding his expectations fulfilled somewhere ... around the next corner, in the next street, the next city, the next country. His life, as one critic has remarked, "can be read in hotel registers."[7] And if that perpetual wandering gives evidence of a desperate restlessness, it also bears witness to a recurrent revival of hope that perhaps somewhere existed a place he could step into as if into his dreams.

But short of arriving there, reality had to be infused with all the thrill and excitement with which his dreams supplied him. Even in a situation in which one might suppose it to suffice, reality had to be enhanced. Tramping across England and Italy in the first flush of new love, his Istra Nashes, his William Wrenns, his Hayden Charts, and his Olivia Lomonds must, for maximum gratification, imagine themselves knights and ladies dashing through the countryside in some exhilarating adventure. And if, in the first novel, William Wrenn, finally installed within the midst of domestic bliss with his American sweetheart, has dreams that reach no further than a house in New Jersey, in the last novel, Hayden Chart and his new bride breathlessly contemplate the tantalizing prospect of expeditions to Burma, Brazil, and Damascus, and book passage on a steamer sailing "southward from Naples, bound out for Smyrna and Alexandria" (*WSW*, p. 249). By means of this psychological mechanism—of which Carol Kennicott's efforts to brighten the sad desolation. of Gopher Prairie are entirely typical—Lewis charged reality with an enchantment without which it would have been that much more difficult to endure.[8]

This need to embellish quotidian reality is one of a number of manifestations of a process which, at the bottom of Lewis' personality, was his unique way of dealing with the fact of his own existence, the fundamental psychological posture, beneath conscious thought or action, forming his life's operating principle. With the experience of cheerless small town life as unhappy memory and with the experience of an environment that in all relevant respects would be Sauk Centre's happy opposite as ever-renewed anticipation, it was a process marked by perpetual oscillation between dream and reality, hopefulness and disillusionment, yearning focussed, unavoidably disappointed, and always revived. The substance of his dreams would vary, the nature and extent of his frustrations would change, the restoration of his hopes would concentrate on different sorts of fulfillment, but it is within this psychic configuration Lewis's life was lived and whose particular patterns of human conduct his fiction invariably reproduce. And it is within this context the Europe–America conflict was to be formulated and within which it was finally to reach a kind of resolution.

Lewis initiated his literary career, as he was to close it, with the image of a ship. For many young people whose imagination stirred them to resent small town life and whose ambition spurred them to escape it, flight in the early decades of this century meant, as it did for Dreiser's Carrie Meeber and Anderson's George Willard, getting on a train destined for Chicago or Cleveland. But from the start, Lewis's dreams centered on Europe. "Make my way to Europe and travel a few years," he writes in his diary when he is sixteen years old.[9] The hero of his first novel muses:

> But his real object [for strolling along the riverfront] was to ...
> go sailing out into the foam and perilous seas of North River....
> and everywhere the world, to his certain witnessing, was
> turned to crusading, to setting forth in great ships as if it were
> again in the brisk morning of history when the joy of
> adventure possessed the Argonauts.[10]

As *Our Mr. Wrenn* records it nearly ten years later, Lewis in 1904 sailed on a cattleboat for England.[11] The trip was arduous and the fortnight spent in Liverpool not much more pleasant. Two years later, apparently undaunted, he went again, this time visiting London. By observing that "in many forms of enterprise America is ahead of England ... but the people know how to live fuller, richer, quieter lives" he foreshadows what even with later elaboration never exceeded the rather limited way in which the explicit content of his fiction distinguished the two cultures.[12] The more crucial aspect of the event, however, was the disappointment.[13] He seems not to have found England answering to his dreams, an experience conforming to what was already a familiar pattern. His high school days in Sauk Centre had been enlivened by fervent hopes of finding friendship at college. First Oberlin, then Yale proved unsatisfactory.[14] Everywhere experience fell short of expectation, but these repeated encounters with failure never congealed into an emotional force sufficient to quell the regeneration of other, differently directed or differently conceived expectations. If one distinct human impulse is always to underestimate the possible, Lewis must surely be counted among those who tend always to overestimate the possible.

His Europe, never to enter his thinking totally divested of a romantic halo, was from the beginning rarely a reality objectively considered but an object of vague desires and dreams which neither the observed actuality could completely contradict nor his own maturity entirely dismiss. It is why he so often appeals to the European past, a medieval and chivalric Europe, or a Europe as incarnated in a woman, the Dodsworthian "Not Impossible She." But with the Europe, say, which, by the time he was writing *Our Mr. Wrenn*, was soon to be the muddy and bloody terrain of the First World War, or with the Europe which, by the time he was writing *World So Wide*, had recently suffered the ravages of the Second World War, he preferred not to deal. And since the needs of his inner life were answered only by an imaginary Europe, contrasting the actual Europe with his native land (a task attempted with *Dodsworth*) could scarcely result in a rationally reached conclusion in favor of one or the other. Neither as proud patriot nor as determined expatriate was Lewis to resolve that history of discontent which was his life. If a choice was made, and in a real sense it was, we must look for the grounds of that decision (and the possibilities for justifying it) in the recesses of his inner life, the psychic depths where his dreams took shape.

His dream of Europe, as has been suggested, was a specific instance of a more general inclination to invest the commonplace and the mundane with an aura of romantic feeling. Not only does Babbitt's unconscious provide him with a fairy child, but, stirred to waking life, his imagination sends him sailing into downtown Zenith as if over perilous seas. Reflecting their creator's psychology, many of his characters entertain some private dream of personal fulfillment. And this is precisely the psychic characteristic which Lewis proposed (in large part by exemplifying it)[15] as marking what distinguished Americans from the Europeans he encountered in his travels. In this distinction we must look for the reasons behind Lewis's provisional affirmation of the land that bred him. That in Gopher Prairie or in Zenith people needed to cherish a dream or cultivate some private spiritual garden in order to sustain them in the waste of their lives was unfortunate, but, as Sam Dodsworth realizes (at least before his reappearance in *World So Wide*), only America provided the sort of environment in which a personal dream could be given reality. Only its relatively loose social structure provided the freedom. Steeped in tradition, its institutions rigid and stable, Europe could not tolerate such aspirations. But how, in America, to succeed in one's attempts to translate the dream into reality when, bewildered in the face of such slack social organization, so many people had rushed to organize themselves into Rotary Clubs, prayer groups, professional societies, country clubs—in short, all those enclaves in the larger scene which guarded their members' allegiance to their conception of things even more zealously than could the entire weight of European tradition? Answering that question, Lewis was logically led—and not at all mysteriously, or paradoxically, or ironically, as Alfred Kazin believed[16]—to a celebration of a set of solidly middle class values, whose generating principle was always some version of Emersonian self-reliance.

The proposition that America offered the opportunity to cultivate and bring to fruition some private dream—was it a naive estimate of the possibilities America granted its inhabitants? No doubt. Again Lewis succumbed to a romantic dream. As he had yearned for a Europe on the basis of a romantic vision of it, he began to yearn for an America—and found it possible to accept it—only on the basis of an equally romantic dream. When the image of a knight riding to save some damsel in distress no longer served his purposes, the image of a self-reliant pioneer hacking out his destiny in the wilds of the American frontier came to animate his fantasies.[17] "There was a sweet wild smell about her, like sagebrush" (*WSW*, p. 247), Lewis says in the last novel, speaking of the home town girl his hero marries.

That dream, however, also evaporated in the face of reality. Dodsworth, who had closed his European experience with hopes of starting a caravan business in America, appears in *World So Wide*, a permanent exile, living in Florence. Yet he advises young Hayden Chart, the novel's hero, to return to America. Though Lewis seems to have concluded that the pioneer spirit could no longer find concrete or physical expression in America, he seems also to have believed that it could be internalized and find spiritual expression, that is, it could provide the driving force behind the quest for self-discovery, for self-awareness, for pursuing a life of the mind. The internalization of the quest for self-fulfillment should have formed the foundation for his own transcendence of the Europe–America problem. His acute sensitivity to "place" should have dulled as he grew in attaching greater importance to what was internal and subjective. But, though certain elements in his last book indicate that he recognized the problem, that his hopes for happiness had been too exclusively directed on "place," that in fact neither Europe as such nor America as such could answer his need for an environment that might embody the realization of his yearnings, he was too old and tired to act on the knowledge or convincingly to show its results in his fiction.

But as if illustrating that perverse sort of justice with which the notorious suffering of artists is often recompensed, Lewis's never completely abandoned romantic vision of Europe, though it did much to make his life difficult, did much to inform his vision of America with that sense of gritty reality for which he has been so often acclaimed, "the exact sound of a Ford car," for example, "being cranked on a summer morning," as Alfred Kazin has pointed out.[18] The disillusioned romantic hope seems to have left him, as it left Babbitt after waking from his fairy child dreams, acutely sensitive to the material details of American life—the toasters, the cocktail shakers, the alarm clocks. For Babbitt, it was a way of filling up the mental vacuum left by the fading of ephemeral fancies. Deprived of his dream by the ringing of the alarm clock, he finds a substitute satisfaction in the very materiality of this clock, its technical ingenuity and practical utility, and, similarly, in the solid substantiality of his house, his car, the skyscrapers of Zenith. Lewis, in recoil from his disappointed expectations of Europe, found a substitute satisfaction in indignation. To show just how spiritually impoverished the American scene was—an impoverishment betrayed by nothing so much as the fanciful nature of the dreams generated to escape it—he determined with an obstinate dedication to expose the material background of America in all its tangible detail, those minutiae of our national existence never before so accurately observed and never before so suggestively noted that, in addition to reproducing the very texture of our lives, they uncover the very substance of our national psyche: the slap on the back that speaks volumes about our ideas of friendship, the sly business deal that speaks volumes about our ideas of morality—all the visible signs of our internal being.

This was the impact his romantic view of Europe had on his art. Apart from either its function as the opposing term in a cultural debate (as it was in *Dodsworth*) or its function as a sort of refuge where one's last days might be spent (as it was in *World So Wide*), Europe ultimately served him as an imaginative construct which at work in the creative process permitted him to shape an art in which America acquired such reality, such vivid presence, that Americans saw—and still see—themselves as if in a mirror freshly wiped clean.[19] But what he sought for his own emotional gratification, a Europe whose reality might match his dreams, he never found.

The search, ending in the physical and mental deterioration of too much alcohol, had begun enthusiastically enough. "For all his life," Mr. Wrenn, living a cramped life as a minor clerk in a Manhattan manufacturing house, "had been planning a great journey" (*OMW*, p. 3). Though at times he envisions that "Great Traveling of his in the land of Big Business" (*OMW*, p. 29), the utter drabness of his existence leads him to dream of seas and ships and exotic places. "He saw the processional of world brotherhood tramp steadily through the paling sunset; saffron-vestured Mandarin marching by flax-faced Norseman and languid South Sea Islander—the diverse peoples toward whom he had always yearned" (*OMW*, p. 46). Unexpectedly the recipient of nearly a thousand dollars, he acts on his desires and sails on a cattleboat bound for Europe. Reflecting Lewis's own first crossing, the experience is disheartening, but instructive as well. Mr. Wrenn's subsequent comments show that Lewis at times was perfectly aware of his tendencies toward romantic inflation, though not often did that knowledge relieve the pain of the inevitable disappointment. In reference to his shipmates, Mr. Wrenn observes: "'I guess they're like cattlemen—the cattle-ier they are, the more romantic they look, and then when you get to know them, the chief trouble with them is that they're cattlemen'" (*OMW*, p. 99). That "chief trouble" was indeed to prove the chief trouble of Lewis's life, the trouble that reality always insisted on remaining just that.

Having disposed of the sea journey as an experience answering to his romantic dreams, Mr. Wrenn exclaims, seeing Liverpool: "'Gee!'" For "up through the Liverpool streets that ran down to the river, as though through peep-holes slashed straight back into the Middle Ages, his vision plunged, and it wandered unchecked through each street while he hummed: 'Free, free, in Eu-ro-pee, that's me'" (*OMW*, p. 58). Yet, despite the "real quaint flavor," despite his "fancies" for a time contenting him, despite his striking up an acquaintance with Dr. Mittyford, the first of those "foreign colony" figures Lewis was later to satirize as either too artificially European or too stubbornly American, Mr. Wrenn sinks into a loneliness more profound than ever endured at home, where the familiarity of the surroundings had always had the power to assuage it.

Mr. Wrenn is spared a stark confrontation with the dearth of his own inner resources, however, by meeting Istra Nash. Because she seems to embody everything exotic, charming, and exciting, he imagines her a French countess and promptly falls in love. She turns out to be an American, of course, and in her mixture of glib coldness and emotional capriciousness anticipates the bitchy Fran Dodsworth and the frigid Olivia Lomond. Hearing her weep one evening, Wrenn thinks of comforting her with: "'Please let me help you, princess, jus' like I was a knight'" (*OMW*, p. 91). She deserts him suddenly, and his European hopes shattered, Wrenn hastens to America with another dream, the hope of populating the home terrain with a large number of friends: "Now, out there was a blue shading, made by a magic pencil; land, his land, where he was going to become the beloved comrade of all the friends whose likenesses he saw in the white-caps flashing before him" (*OMW*, p. 147). After several initial setbacks, his hope is finally fulfilled. He finds not only a circle of friends but a wholesome wife. Yet, despite his joyful entrance into the human community—active participation in that peculiarly American camaraderie which Babbitt, at the cost of whatever ideals he began to glimpse, could not do without, and which for Lewis stood in irreconcilable conflict with the equally peculiarly American aspirations toward self-reliance—the romantic yearning cannot be suppressed. "'The people here,'" he sighs, "'are awful kind and good, and you can bank on 'em. But—oh—'" (*OMW*, p. 235). Exclaimed again and again in the course of Lewis's career, this "oh" of longing was less and less echoed by the "Gee!" of discovery and more and more answered by the drink that would dull the pain of frustration.

In its array of secondary characters, in the patterns of human experience established by their reciprocal relationships, and in its hero's passage through progressive disillusionment to some mostly unformulated and inarticulated hope to be satisfied in the future somehow, *Our Mr. Wrenn* heralds in a skeletal way the entire form and substance of the experiential area with which Lewis was subsequently to deal, and for that reason, for its quality of innocent unselfconsciousness, can be seen as a direct transcription of Lewis's psychic life, a guileless disclosure of the essential forces determining the choice of his material and the way he was typically to shape it. The tone would acquire more sophistication, the content of his novels more thoughtfulness, but Europe was never completely to be stripped of the romantic aura with which he habitually surrounded it.

In *Dodsworth*, however, no doubt partly as a result of his extended stays there and partly as the result of his own maturity, Europe did become a term in a cultural dialectic less obviously influenced by emotion. Though, perhaps, the explicitly expressed comparisons between Europe and America rarely transcended the superficial—fireplaces against central heating, for example—who would deny that most of us lead lives at just that level? For someone like Lewis, someone not especially interested in or capable of understanding the substructures of personal, cultural, or political value ultimately responsible for the differences in manner, style, or custom, these differences alone will suffice to offer an authentic basis for comparison and, eventually, an irreproachable foundation for the expression of preference. The reasons Sam Dodsworth uses to explain his permanent removal to Florence in *World So Wide* sound not merely a little silly but even a little vulgar when, for instance, he contrasts the hateful servants in America with their contented counterparts in Europe. Yet his reasons make perfect sense when one grants him (and Lewis) the subjective nature of his appraisal. Without reference to personal preference, whether America marked an advance or a decline from European culture was never a question Lewis tried seriously to answer. Apart from what is somewhat lamely concluded at the close of *Dodsworth*, Lewis never went very far to solve the problem his own "European" books posed, that is, which culture held a higher conception of the human spirit, and which, as a result, afforded the climate least likely to impede the fullest possible expression of human potential.

His reactions to Europe, as to America, were immediate, instinctive, and inevitably conditioned by his emotional needs. However, this gives us no cause to dismiss his reactions from serious attention, for his emotional needs and the various evaluations of Europe derived from his success or failure to satisfy them there were far from idiosyncratic. In fact, so typical were they that they happened to sum up how many sensitive and intelligent Americans were coming to feel about Europe—the feeling, justified or not, that in happy contrast to so many aspects of American life seemingly deliberately calculated to irritate a reasonably cultivated person, Europe furnished an aesthetically pleasing, morally sophisticated, and generally favorable environment for the pursuit and discovery of an authentic life. When Lewis succeeded with Sam Dodsworth in creating a character not completely under the spell of his romantic fantasies, it is in the main this vision of Europe which draws him.

In his last book Lewis would characterize Europe as acting like a drug for Americans, "'so lulling after our brisk, raw climate at home, where we have to face the blizzard, fight through it or freeze'" (*WSW*, p. 140). It was his way, when old and sick, of recommending the pioneer spirit to his young hero, Hayden Chart. But at moments when Europe did not primarily serve as an object of romantic hopes and before it began to serve, both literally and figuratively, as merely a soothing locale, a sort of sanctuary in which to endure the disillusions of a lifetime, Lewis did confront in an objective way the relationship between the two cultures.

"'Certainly like to see Europe some day. When I graduated, I thought I'd be a civil engineer and see the Brazil jungle and China and all over.... But Certainly going to see Europe, anyway,'"[20] decides Sam Dodsworth at the start of a career and a marriage which will postpone the fulfillment of his wish for several decades. Only after he relinquishes control of his business does the vision of himself as a Richard Harding Davis hero return: "Riding a mountain trail, two thousand sheer feet above a steaming valley; sun-helmet and whipcord breeches; tropical rain on a tin-roofed shack; a shot in the darkness as he sat over a square-face of gin with a ragged tramp of Noble Ancestry" (*D*, p. 13). Now fifty, echoing Babbitt's complaint, he feels cheated of his own life by having behaved in strict conformity to the expectations of others. Unlike Babbitt, however, whose need for backslapping comradeship much outweighs the need for self-discovery or self-assertion, Dodsworth finds himself robbed of the "pride in pioneering which was one of his props in life" (*D*, p. 22). Dodsworth does possess a self. Denied the opportunity to grow freely and naturally from the core of his being, however, it is a false self, one imposed on him by his role as president of the Revelation Automobile Company. Stripped of that role, he feels lost, empty, and faceless. His gnawing sense of discontent, not so radical as to suggest to him that his life has been wasted, does suggest that he has missed something, something vital and essential, a chance to explore his own nature at his own leisure in the surroundings he dreamed of when young.

This particular emotional state—the desire to pursue the realization of half-buried longings because daily life no longer satisfies—generates most of the action in most of Lewis's fiction, whether, as in *Dodsworth* and the two other "European" novels, as a point from which the action develops, or, as in *Babbitt*, as a point to which it leads. Certainly one of his own most characteristic emotional conditions, Lewis saw it, probably correctly, as constituting a uniquely American frame of mind. As *Dodsworth* repeats again and again, the demands of "daily life" in America are so heavily dominated by the Puritan work ethic—a cultural dictum which, when obeyed, provides no time for the unhurried discovery of selfhood and fewer and fewer opportunities for the expression of that selfhood—that our dreams, though suppressed in our everyday dealings with each other, acquire in the depths of our psychic life a degree of intensity they would never attain in another culture. In a sense, then, much of the cross-cultural chatter in *Dodsworth* is superfluous, for Sam himself, as "dreamer," emerges as entirely representative of the American mind, and, given the nature of that mind, personifies a considerable criticism of American life. Nothing, in short, attests to the spiritually deadening nature of our national life as our need for such dreams of self-fulfillment. As he himself acknowledges, Sam's career has left him "spiritually rheumatic."

Sam's yearnings draw him to Europe. What does he find? At once he finds a lot of talk. Distilled, these conversations concerning the

America–Europe question would sound somewhat like this: American life is crude, hectic, standardized, and devoid of privacy. Americans themselves are not interested in anything except accusing those who are not "Doing Something Important" of grave sins against humanity. European life, on the other hand, is easier, slower, more human. And Europeans, mellowed by tradition, are more gracious, polite, and kind. And if Americans are more hearty, more earthy, Sam learns in his experience with Nande Azeredo that Europeans can be too. In a lecture whose Nietzschean drift one suspects Lewis to have derived from H. L. Mencken, Professor Braut sums up a crucial difference:

> 'The European culture is aristocratic.... as against democratic, in that we believe that the nation is proudest and noblest and most exalted which has the greatest number of really great men ... and that ordinary ... people ... are happier in contributing to produce such great men than in having more automobiles and bath-tubs.' (D, p. 231)

But because the distinction has to do with something as fundamental as man's relationship to nature, it is Edith Cortright who voices what Lewis himself must have regarded as the most significant difference between the two cultures. Europeans are mystics, Mrs. Cortright maintains: "'They love earth and wind and rain and sun.... That's the strength of Europe ... its nearness to earth'" (D, p. 335). And the weakness of America lies in its having directed all its energies to insulate people from the natural world. On the one hand, to increase our material comfort, we manipulate nature for exclusively practical ends, and, on the other hand, nevertheless craving spiritual comfort, we indulge ourselves in extravagant dreams of escape from the unnatural world we have created, missing that whole area of experience located between these two extremes: quiet cultivation of our capacity to take joy in ourselves and others, to extract pleasure from what nature permits us, to accept reality as it is found, and, on that basis, to bring to light the secret which is peace of body and mind.

That this idea represents no particularly novel criticism of American life does not diminish its validity. Having become aware of it, Sam Dodsworth will choose, one would expect, to end his days in Europe. But among the lessons Europe has taught him is the one which tells him that he is, after all, an American. As Elon Richards says: "'And you, Sam, you old grizzly, can never be a contemplative gazelle. You've got to fight'" (D, p. 161). Groping to find something in America worthy of affirmation, Sam appeals to the American past. He remembers Old Pop Conover, a Pony

Express Rider in his youth, to whom it never occurred that he was any better than the tramp or any worse than a king'" (*D*, p. 156). Sam concludes: "'He was a real American'" (*D*, p. 156). Edith supports him: "'But I am sure that there is still a sturdy, native America—and not Puritanical, either'" (*D*, p. 314). Finally, in response to one of Fran's silly remarks about "tradition," Sam "thought of the tradition of pioneers pushing to the westward, across the Alleghenies, through the forests of Kentucky and Tennessee, on to the bleeding plains of Kansas, on to Oregon and California, a religious procession ..." (*D*, p. 327). Digging at the roots of the American character, Sam uncovers an image of it inspired by visions of the frontier.

So strong a hold has this pioneer-grappling-with-the-frontier complex of ideas exercised over the imagination of Americans that it could be pointed to as forming our national myth, our version of that primal encounter between man and universe in which a national soul is forged. No doubt the confrontation between vigorous men and virgin territory has moved the American mind so profoundly because in raising our young voice against the authority of Europe we have envisioned that encounter between frontier and pioneer to demand the tapping of inner resources as spiritually exalted as those which erected Gothic cathedrals or painted the ceilings of papal chapels.

Finding his own active character perfectly in tune with what his European experience has taught him about the core of the American character, Sam decides to return to America. He has answered the question posed at the start of his journey—"Is America the Rome of the world, or is it inferior to Britain and Europe? or confusedly both?" (*D*, p. 92)—but in such extremely personal terms that the answer cannot lay claim to general validity. Seeing a group of fascists boating on the Bay of Naples—a sight that might have led him to consider Europe's apparent amenability to the kind of thinking fascism represents, especially in connection with what he heard Professor Braut say of Europe's anti-democratic bias—he ignores them. The spectacle does "not suit his romantic private vision of the Bay of Naples" (*D*, p. 331). Needless to say, he turns to America on the strength of an equally romantic vision. The real problem had always been for him, as it was for Lewis, the one with which Elon Richards confronts him: "'For Heaven's sake decide whether you, your own self, are happier in America or in Europe, and then stick there!'" (*D*, p. 162). Less a matter of deciding which culture, given some standard of evaluation, was better, it was more a matter of deciding which culture, given a certain personality, offered an environment responsive to the particular needs of that personality.

As if somehow to duplicate the exhilarating image of Conestoga wagons rolling across the plains, Sam dreams of manufacturing caravans.

With what we now know of trailer parks, littered campgrounds, scenery spoiled, and nature almost everywhere ravished, we finish reading *Dodsworth* uncomfortably aware that Sam's dream is as financially astute as it is spiritually base. Even from Sam's own perspective, the caravan would seem a pathetic diminution of a venerable symbol of courage, endurance, and the search for freedom. It is hard to resist believing it Lewis's own unwitting admission that without a real frontier, an actual physical frontier to engage the active vigor of Americans, the pioneer spirit becomes susceptible to gross misapplication and misdirection. Though this spirit may issue in the planning and execution of projects in some way analogous to the settling of the frontier, they inevitably violate its essence. Sam associates the westward movement with freedom, a concept his European experience has helped him to value highly, but what one associates with traveling caravans is aimless wandering, freedom untempered by purpose or goal. The image suggests escape, but an escape which, unlike the pioneer spirit as it informed American thinking in the last century, presupposes no alternative to the situation instigating the escape. Lewis reveals here, probably contrary to his intentions, that once broken free of American society, one is condemned, in the absence of an actual frontier to occupy one's energies, to wander in a sort of psychic wilderness.

The problem was that Lewis failed to discover in modern industrial America a field of activity authentically equivalent to that which had sustained the pioneer spirit. Certainly Hayden Chart's project to build a prairie village "housed in one skyscraper: the first solution in history of rural isolation and loneliness" (*WSW*, p. 9) is no more appropriate than a caravan to signify a genuine resurrection of the pioneer spirit. One is led to suspect Lewis, despite himself, acknowledging that no such field of activity existed in twentieth century America. In other words, the typical American dream of self-fulfillment, so much more intensely adhered to on this continent than in Europe because of the nature of American reality, is a yearning that strives for no more than simple escape, which, once effected, may leave one free, but also leaves one lost.

Hayden Chart in Lewis's last book, *World So Wide*, registers this sense of bewilderment most strongly. If William Wrenn and Sam Dodsworth headed for Europe with some measure of eager anticipation, Hayden begins his journey in a mood much less hopeful, feeling himself "desolatingly free to wander in a world too bleakly, too intimidatingly wide" (*WSW*, p. 11). Though he too, like Wrenn and Dodsworth, is a captive of romantic fancies, he fears: " 'I shall never be that romantic wanderer, that troubadour in a ribbon-tied jeep singing through Provence' " (*WSW*, p. 20). There is a note of desperation detectable here that is not present in *Our Mr. Wrenn* and *Dodsworth*. It is the kind of desperation which intimates the presence of a serious intention, the seriousness of the problem creating the expectation of a solution equally seriously conceived.

In *Our Mr. Wrenn*, Europe was presented almost exclusively as an object of romantic hopes and dismissed as soon as those hopes proved misplaced. *Dodsworth* presents Europe, beyond its function as an object of romantic hopes, as constituting a real alternative culture, one of whose effects, despite its intrinsic merits, was to disclose the equally persuasive merits of American culture, and, what Lewis believed to be its driving force, the pioneer spirit. And, since only in America could the pioneer spirit be given full expression, Europe's ultimate effect was to redirect the would-be expatriate's hopes back to America. But these hopes also proved false. Because of the particular relationship between American public life and its citizens' private dreams, only the fervent desire to escape informed those dreams, and, as such, marked a degeneration or perversion of the pioneer spirit.

The solution Lewis found, given the desperate dilemma of an eroded self facing its own psychic waste, was to envisage the pioneering dream as having to include not merely the urge to explore physical landscape but the urge to explore the inner landscape of mind. For that reason, the real intent of Hayden Chart's journey to Europe, as he himself confesses, "'is less to voyage in any geographical land than travel in my own self'" (*WSW*, p. 28). As a result, the journey to Europe is made not because Europe is Europe, but because Europe simply offers an alien environment, a setting which, failing to reinforce one's customary identity, furnishes the opportunity to establish the self on grounds more authentic than the expectations of one's neighbors and compatriots: "'I must voyage away from everybody who is familiar with the shape of my nose and the contents of my checkbook, find a world where I've never seen a soul, and so find some one who knows what I'm really like— and who will tell *me*, because I'd be interested to learn!'" (*WSW*, p. 28). Having opened with the urge toward self-discovery, the novel closes with Hayden Chart convinced he has begun to know himself.

Unfortunately, Lewis did not possess an especially introspective turn of mind and, consequently, had no power to demonstrate a character such as Hayden Chart's growing self-knowledge. The novel's serious impulse is almost totally compromised. It is a sad fact that just as one detects in Lewis the beginnings of knowing what he had pursued all these years, the knowledge that the urge toward self-discovery is man's noblest urge and the life of the mind which this presupposes the ideal life, whether practiced in Gopher Prairie, Florence, or anywhere else, he was simply growing too old and exhausted to make the idea convincing, for nothing in *World So Wide* suggests that Hayden Chart has indeed begun to know himself, and by virtue of that knowledge to dismiss the Europe–America question as irrelevant.[21]

Writing about *Babbitt* in 1931, George Santayana alluded to what he called Lewis's "prophetic intention," regretting, however, that in the work "no suggestion of the direction appears in which salvation may come."[22] However shakily, by the end of his career Lewis was indeed pointing out such a direction. And, curiously, it was a direction Santayana himself had designated almost forty years earlier as leading to America's salvation when, addressing an audience in California, he concluded that "the interest and beauty of this inner landscape, rather than any fortunes that may await his body in the outer world, constitute [man's] proper happiness."[23] Lewis seems to have been moving toward solving the dilemma his "European" books dramatized in a way strikingly similar, namely, by proposing that physical environment and social or cultural climate cease to be of much importance when one is securely in possession of a solid and deeply comprehended sense of self. Aware, however, that Americans in general did not often face up to the challenge of an internalized life, Lewis has Hayden Chart, at the end of *World So Wide*, planning tours to Ceylon, India, and Japan—and thereby suggesting that this compelling urge to travel characterizes Americans as not yet having dreams which involve more than simple escape.

Though the tone has changed from youthful hope in escape's beneficial effects—Wrenn returns to America eager to embrace it; Babbitt returns to Zenith after his rest in the Maine woods full of "pep"—to a rueful admission that escape so perceived is a deficient concept, Lewis ends where he began, irresistibly drawn by the lure of the strange and the faraway. Nonetheless, we cannot finish reading *World So Wide* without discerning in Lewis the faint appearance of a hope that it is possible for Americans to transcend their febrile oscillation between the dispiriting nature of their daily lives and the dreams of escape it gives rise to by pursuing a life of the mind, which as a sort of fresh frontier might summon forth all the daring, all the courage, all the exalted nobility he associated with the pioneer spirit. In this way, America might indeed become "the Rome of the world."

Finally, then, Lewis's romantic dreams, indisputably adolescent, inevitably frustrated, did issue in—and are somehow validated by—a vision of America which, however direly glimpsed and weakly articulated, was at bottom maturely conceived, a vision no longer the result of fanciful dreams but the result of a struggle to define an ideal, a vision which, proceeding from our actual past could point to an actual future, a vision of a potential America whose realization might be unlikely but whose inspiration would immeasurably improve the quality of American life. If in his imagination, if not in his person, Lewis did ultimately affirm America, he did so on the basis of that ideal vision of its possibilities. Though no "promised land," America remained for Lewis the land of promise.

Meanwhile, Europe, no longer significant for him as a place either where one's dreams of a romantic life might be enacted or where a genuine alternative culture had its life, became for him a sort of asylum, a retreat where weary Americans like Sam Dodsworth (and himself) could drift toward death with a minimal amount of external disturbance.

NOTES

1. *Abinger Harvest* (London, 1936), p. 127.

2. Two years earlier, under the pseudonym of Tom Graham, Lewis had published *Hike and the Aeroplane*, an adventure story for boys. Strictly speaking, this must of course be considered his first book.

3. That is, the twenties, which saw the publication of all the works responsible for his reputation and which culminated in his winning the Nobel Prize for Literature in 1930.

4. "The American Scholar," *The Works of Ralph Waldo Emerson* (Boston, 1909), I, 113.

5. James Lundquist, *Sinclair Lewis* (New York, 1973), p. 6.

6. *World So Wide* (New York, 1951), pp. 240–241, Further references in the text will be preceded by *WSW*.

7. Lundquist, p. 24.

8. Responding to this aspect of Carol Kennicott's character and attempting to situate it within an important tradition, Martin Light (in "The Quixotic Motifs of *Main Street*," *Arizona Quarterly*, XXIX, Autumn, 1973, p. 221) calls Carol, as Harry Levin had called Emma Bovary, a type of the "female quixote." Not only astute with respect to *Main Street*, the observation provides a suggestive viewpoint from which to regard the entirety of Lewis's fiction.

9. Quoted in Mark Schorer, *Sinclair Lewis: An American Life* (New York, 1961), p. 28.

10. *Our Mr. Wrenn* (New York, 1914), p. 8. Further references in the text will be preceded by *OMW*.

11. Schorer, pp. 79–80.

12. Schorer, pp. 109–110.

13. More crucial because to emotional reactions such as this Lewis's inability to manage more rigorously intellectual comparisons can in large part be attributed.

14. Schorer, pp. 54, 66.

15. It was no whim of Mark Schorer to subtitle his biography of Lewis *An American Life*. He meant to suggest that Lewis's character embodied in a highly representative way traits uniquely typical of the national character.

16. *On Native Grounds* (Garden City, N.Y., 1956), p. 174.

17. For a fuller discussion of the pioneer image in Lewis, see Glen A. Love's "New Pioneering on the Prairies: Nature, Progress and the Individual in the Novels of Sinclair Lewis," *American Quarterly*, XXV (Dec., 1973), pp. 558–577.

18. Kazin, p. 176.

19. Lewis's satiric intentions, often at cross purposes between the derision he brought to what America was and the hope he brought to what it could be, prevent that reflected image, however, from being as evaluatively clear as it is visually clear.

20. *Dodsworth* (New York, 1967), p. 12. Further references in the text will be preceded by *D*.

21. The failure here is one more example of Lewis's central problem as a novelist, his apparently irresistible propensity to resolve the intellectual problems his books pose on terms predominantly emotional. We can be happy with William Wrenn, with Sam Dodsworth, with Hayden Chart for finding "the right woman," but love is neither an adequate nor an appropriate solution to the sociological and psychological issues Lewis raises.

22. *The Letters of George Santayana*, ed. Daniel Cory (London, 1955), p. 265.

23. "The Genteel Tradition in American Philosophy," *The Genteel Tradition: Nine Essays by George Santayana*, ed. Douglas Wilson (Cambridge, Mass., 1964), p. 64.

BEA KNODEL

For Better or for Worse ...

Sinclair Lewis, in the novels of his most satisfactorily productive decade, the 1920s, looks critically but often with incisive clarity at American life. In portraying the vulgarity and stultifying narrowness of the small town as exemplified by Gopher Prairie, the essential emptiness of the life of George F. Babbitt, or the yearning and self-searchings of Sam Dodsworth as he measures the American experience against the European, Lewis was also portraying marriages—occasionally happy marriages, many humdrum marriages, and some utterly wretched marriages—and in the process he made some telling comments about what marriage meant to American wives in the first quarter of the twentieth century.

If it is true, as Daniel Aaron has said, that *Main Street* is "a work of historical importance ... not merely as a reflection partly unconscious, of American tastes and assumptions, but also because it helped Americans to understand themselves" (177); if *The New York Times* saw the central character in *Babbitt* as "real, alive and recognizable as a known, familiar, and abundant type" (Schorer 345); and if in *Dodsworth* Lewis presented once again a representative type of American, "the American boy-man, the 'mythical' archetype" (Moore 160), it then seems fair to use these three novels as a means of seeing into a time now gone and of examining the lives of women in that vanished time. Happy wives are not much seen in *Main*

From *Modern Fiction Studies* 31, Issue 3 (1985). © 1985 by the Purdue Research Foundation.

Street, *Babbitt*, and *Dodsworth*. Occasionally, there are wives who at least appear to enjoy their lives and their marriages; and there are two, Vida Sherwin Wutherspoon and Bea Sorenson Bjornstam (both in *Main Street*), who are most definitely, most radiantly married.

It may be, of course, that some of the wives who appear to be happy are simply not unhappy, an entirely different thing; but there is a quality of enjoyment of life in women such as Juanita Haydock (*Main Street*) and Matey Pearson (*Dodsworth*) that seems to argue that they find their days, their husbands, and their own roles satisfactory enough.

Juanita is described as "acidulous and shrewd and cackling" (242). Her home, carefully detailed by Lewis, is new, an overheated concrete bungalow, furnished to a pitch of Gopher Prairie fashion, and she herself is "highly advanced in the matters of finger-bowls, doilies, and bath mats" (90). That she sees herself as having achieved distinction as the leading light of the Young Married Set, Lewis assures us; that she sees any reason to question the absolute significance of that achievement, we are nowhere led to believe. She accepts the limitations of Gopher Prairie because she does not recognize it as having limitations. She enjoys the summers at the lake, the squabbles with the grocer, and the social eminence of the Jolly Seventeen. She is, in short, satisfied.

Matey Pearson, the wife of Sam Dodsworth's longtime friend Tub, is, in almost every particular, vastly different from Juanita Haydock; but Matey, like Juanita, has apparently found happiness in an acceptance of things as they are. Fran Dodsworth may dismiss Matey as "dreadfully uninteresting. And fat!" (257), but Matey plays "a rare shrewd game of poker" (263), dances lightly, grows Zenith's most admirable dahlias, and shows herself cheerfully affectionate toward her husband, whom she says, with apparent truth, she, adores. Lewis does not show us many details in the lives of Juanita and Matey or of other women who appear to find their lives and their marriages satisfactory, but the glimpses he does reveal are of pleasures enjoyed, not of dull boredom or lonely pain.

Lewis goes much further, however, in showing the possibilities for wives' finding happiness when, in *Main Street*, he describes the marriages of Vida Sherwin and Bea Sorenson. And because, Tolstoy's remark to the contrary, all happy families are not alike, it is worthwhile to explore in some detail the reasons why Vida and Bea are so happily married.

Vida is thirty-nine years old when she marries Raymie Wutherspoon, and she has behind her long years of struggling with sexual "fears, longing and guilt" (244), of knowing she is perceived as plain, the stereotypical old maid schoolteacher, of making her home in boarding houses. For Vida, then, marriage means, among other things, having what no "nice" single woman in a small town in 1915 could have—a sex life. And Lewis, though he is the least likely of authors to attempt to paint an explicit sexual scene, assures the reader that after her marriage Vida becomes "daily and visibly more plump" (264), happier, more self-assured, while her husband, Raymie, glows and feels masculine as he thinks of "the tempestuous surprises of love revealed by Vida" (254). Further, Vida has her own home "after detached brown years in boarding houses" (255), and she triumphs in her new life, her status.

Bea Sorenson, after her marriage to Miles Bjornstam, is even happier, if possible, than the married Vida Sherwin, Bea is happy first because she loves Miles. He has, after all, enough appeal to have been able to charm even the fastidious Carol Kennicott, and to Bea he is indeed a Swedish Othello with adventures to tell and with a wealth of devotion to give. Beyond that, Bea, unlike any of the other wives to be discussed, is by class and by upbringing content to do domestic work and positively delighted to do it in her own home instead of as a hired girl in someone else's. And finally—and this is significant—she finds excitement and creativity in each household task because she is "Miles's *full partner*" (308, italics mine). Here is a key; it is because she is her husband's full partner that her work has significance and meaning to her.

In the less-than-happy marriages Lewis portrays in *Main Street*, *Babbitt*, and *Dodsworth*, it is commonplace that the wives, even when they are much loved, and some of them are, are in no real sense their husbands' partners. We see the woman who is deliberately humiliated, kept in her place, by her husband; the woman who has, in most respects, ceased to exist for her husband; and often, the woman who has been effectively crippled, by being permitted, or even required, to remain irresponsible, immature, and selfish. The relationships between men and women, husbands and wives, in the years about which Lewis is writing, the years from 1910 to 1925 or so, were obviously established by the attitudes of the time; and he is reporting what he has seen. But he does not let it go at that. He seeks reasons and explanations for the dissatisfaction of the women he portrays; and, with one notable exception, he is ready to offer some word of defense for even the silliest or most disagreeable unhappy wife. He is, in fact, essentially sympathetic.

He pictures with feeling the humiliation of the woman totally dependent on her husband for money. In a moving scene, one that many readers may still recognize, he shows Maud Dyer (*Main Street*) asking her husband in front of an appreciative male audience at the corner drugstore for ten dollars to buy underclothes for her (and his) children, only to have him ask, as both the listening Carol Kennicott and the reader know he will, "Where's that ten dollars I gave you last year?" (74). When Maud is shown later as a rather silly hypochondriac, interested in religious experiments and in the possibility of seducing Will Kennicott, Lewis has provided if not an excuse for her behavior at least a suggestion as to its possible causes.

And he is sympathetic to Edith Cortright (*Dodsworth*), who, describing her deceased husband, says he was

> a dreadful liar; one of these hand-kissing, smiling, convincing liars. He was a secret drunkard. He humiliated me constantly as a backwoods American; used to apologize to people, oh, so prettily, when I said "I guess" instead of the equally silly "I fancy." (322)

Mrs. Cortright, because she is nearly perfect, needs no excuses, but she most decidedly has Lewis' compassion.

More in need of excuses is Louetta Swanson (*Babbitt*), whose snappishness and flirtations are the responses of a woman who is also publicly embarrassed by her husband and privately bored and dissatisfied. At a dinner at the Babbitts in a scene that is presumably representative, Eddie Swanson complains at length about Louetta's new dress, which is "top short, too low, too immodestly thin, and much too expensive" (102). It is small wonder that Louetta rages back. Lewis has additionally introduced their quarrel with a description of the emptiness of Louetta's life and of the lives of women like her—lives made vain and purposeless almost by decree:

> In Floral Heights and the other prosperous sections of Zenith, especially in the "young married set," there were many women who had nothing to do. Though they had few servants, yet with gas stove, electric ranges and dishwashers and vacuum cleaners, and tiled kitchen walls, their homes were so convenient that they had little housework, and much of their food came from bakeries and delicatessens. They had but two, one, or no children; and despite the myth that the Great War had made work respectable, their husbands objected to their "wasting time and getting a lot of crank ideas" in unpaid social work, and still more to their causing a rumor, by earning money, that their were not adequately supported. (102)

Thus the reader is prepared for Louetta's behavior and may in some measure understand it.

Lewis touches honestly but with surprising, gentleness on the life of Louetta's neighbor, that matronly housewife Myra Babbitt, a woman so dull that no one with the possible exception of her ten-year-old daughter is even aware of her existence. She is vacuous; she is apparently nearly without either active intelligence or self-esteem. The reader sees her reading in the daily paper only the headlines, the society pages (wistfully) and the department store ads; apologizing to her husband for his hangover; exulting over the deliciousness of fried chicken served to dinner guests. Lewis comments that "... one of Mrs. Babbitt's virtues was that ... she took care of the house, and didn't bother the males by thinking" (72).

It is only near the end of the novel, when her husband has been immersed in his own attempts at rebellion and in his love affair, that he begins "to see her as a human being; to like and dislike her instead of accepting her as a comparatively movable part of the furniture" (280). And it is only then that Lewis, though he never tells what Myra is thinking, permits her to describe her life—ordering three meals a day, everyday; sewing; shopping. Further, he shows with flaring satire but also with a touch of pathos the utter hopelessness of her attempt to find intellectual stimulus, "inspiration for the New Era," by going to hear Mrs. Opal Emerson Mudge, field-lecturer, for the American New Thought League, speak on "Cultivating the Sun Spirit" (284).

The disasters that may be caused by restricting women's independence, intellectual activity, and maturity are shown by Lewis to go beyond the nagging and casual flirting of Louetta Swanson or the inarticulate unhappiness of Myra Babbitt. They may, for one thing, lead to the total collapse of a marriage, a more dramatic event in 1920 than in 1985. In *Dodsworth* Lewis presents the one unhappy wife for whom he shows no sympathy—the beautiful, mercurial, absolute bitch Fran—and shows her as she destroys her marriage and to some extent herself.

Fran Dodsworth is the classic character that readers love to hate. She is, of course, patterned on Lewis' first wife, Grace Hegger; and Lewis was writing *Dodsworth* at the time his marriage had just broken up. Nonetheless he, inadvertently no doubt, introduces some elements into his writing about Fran that reveal her, her husband, and the era in which they live in such a way that a reader can feel, if not sympathy, at least a bit of understanding for Fran.

Like so many of the wives Lewis describes, but at a different social level, Fran Dodsworth has been effectively stunted by the attitudes of society and even of the man—and in this case he is a kind, intelligent man—who loves her. Sam, for all that he adores Fran, thinks of her as a child, "his child" (52); and it is not until he meets the woman for whom he will eventually leave Fran that "his child" becomes, less attractively, "childish." In response to his insistence that she is "so young," "a child," "a girl," it is no wonder that Fran, though she is in her forties, talks baby talk; lies, even to Sam, about her age; hides the fact that she is a grandmother. Sam comes gradually to see her as shallow, but he never acknowledges that the causes of her shallowness may lie outside her control; that his continually thinking of her as a child may have contributed to making her irresponsible; that with her life occupied by clubs that, in her own words, "don't mean anything" but are "just make believe" (19), with no purpose other than keeping her occupied, she has had little incentive to grow; that if he finds himself uncertain of his identity when he is no longer recognized as an important figure in the auto industry, she, whom he has resolved to keep in a shrine, who has never had work for which she might be recognized, may well have little clear sense of herself as a person.

Nor in this instance does Lewis step in to offer excuses. In fact he also keeps Fran firmly in her place. It is not just that he delineates her bitchiness with such unremitting effectiveness. He also minimizes her. From the opening paragraphs of the novel in which Sam Dodsworth's "massive" head is juxtaposed against the "little smiling heads" (9) of the girls dancing on the porch of the Kennepoose Canoe Club (with just the suggestion of massive brain power juxtaposed with very little), Fran is insistently denigrated, though often in the nicest possible way. She chatters, she whimpers, she is slight and little and small. She is, in the final analysis, not quite a real person; not, in spite of her husband's love for her, significant.

Even Zilla Riesling, that shrillest of harpies, the wife of George Babbitt's friend Paul, fares better at Lewis' hands than does Fran Dodsworth. Zilla is dreadful, so dreadful that Paul, finally too far driven, shoots her, and readers are invited to be sympathetic to Paul. But Lewis provides Zilla with a defender. It is, in fact, Myra Babbitt who says, "Poor Zilla, she's so unhappy. She takes it out on Paul. She hasn't a single thing to do in that little flat. And she broods too much. And she used to be so pretty and gay, and she resents losing it" (114).

Lewis is understanding, at least generally, of the woman trapped in a life without meaning. And his greatest sympathy he reserves for the "woman with a working brain and no work" (86), most clearly exemplified by Carol Kennicott (*Main Street*). Lewis' treatment of Carol is different from his treatment of the other wives in his novels. Although he never tells the reader what Myra Babbitt or Zilla Riesling or Fran Dodsworth is thinking, throughout most of *Main Street* Lewis presents Carol's point of view, Carol's thoughts. Carol is different, also, from the other wives, except Vida Sherwin, in that she has gone to college; and if Blodgett College is not Dodsworth's Yale, nor even Babbitt's State U, still Carol has been exposed to higher education and has even independently earned her own living. Once married, however, Carol loses most of her independence. Although Kennicott is a loving husband and honestly means to be fair, he never manages to establish a household allowance for his wife, and Carol is often in the absolutely dependent position of having to ask for money. At the same time, she finds that she has little opportunity for productive use of her intelligence or her imaginative or creative powers. That she cannot, as the wife of a professional man, have a career of her own is understood, and although she makes repeated attempts to find fulfillment in her husband's work, to make a career of being the doctor's wife; she finds that unsatisfactory. She even seeks, ludicrously, to create meaning for herself by taking interest in her husband's hobbies, but she concludes finally that "It isn't enough, to stand by while he fills an automobile radiator and chucks me bits of information" (196). With no opportunity for meaningful work apart from her home and family or for the dignity of financial self-sufficiency, Carol is effectively trapped.

The fact that Lewis' vision of Carol's dilemma is clear is verified by the letters he received, "scores" according to his biographer Mark Schorer (269), from women who saw themselves as "Carol Kennicotts." And the dilemma remains unresolved at the end of the novel; perhaps it is incapable of resolution. Lewis sees the problem, analyzes it, and finally, as has been often noted, gives Will Kennicott, the practical voice, the husband's voice, the last word.

In 1961 Schorer wrote an Afterword for *Main Street*: "Today when emancipation of women, for better or worse, is an accomplished fact ... we can, perhaps, read *Main Sheet* only as one reads a historical novel" (434). The comment is still applicable in the mid-1980s and is applicable, as well, to *Babbitt* and *Dodsworth*, both firmly set in the early decades of the century. But Schorer's word "only" is deceptive. We can look at history through historical novels; and we can see how much or how little has changed. Certainly it is respectable now for wives to have both jobs and careers. Certainly women are going to college, in greater numbers now than men. There are women in Babbitt's state universities, women in Dodsworth's Ivy League, women doctors, and women, realtors. But it is still worthwhile to examine our history, to see through fiction the effects that attitudes can have, and through remembering the past to avoid repeating it.

WORKS CITED

Aaron, Daniel. "Sinclair Lewis: *Main Street*." *The American Novel from James Fenimore Cooper to William Faulkner*. Ed. Wallace Stegner. New York: Basic, 1965. 166–179.
Lewis, Sinclair. *Babbitt*. 1922. New York: NAL, 1961.
———. *Dodsworth*. 1929. New York: NAL, 1961.
———. *Main Street*. 1920. New York: NAL, 1961.

Moore, Geoffrey. "Sinclair Lewis: A Lost Romantic." *Sinclair Lewis: A Collation of Critical Essays*. Ed. Mark Schorer. Englewood Cliffs: Prentice, 1962. 151–165.

Schorer, Mark. Afterword. *Main Street*. New York: NAL, 1961. 433–439.

———. *Sinclair Lewis: An American Life*. New York: McGraw, 1961.

DAVID G. PUGH*

Baedekers, Babbittry, and Baudelaire

If T. S. Eliot published a Baedeker's Guide to the landmarks of a spiritual wasteland in 1922, then the same year Sinclair Lewis constructed a sociologist's Ideal-Type to analyze a cultural wasteland, both on Main Street in small-town Gopher Prairie and in Zip City, George F. Babbitt's Zenith, Winnemac, U.S.A. The first one-fourth of the novel closely follows Babbitt's daily routines and rituals, as the individual's symbolic behavior surfaces in his use of artifacts and in his social contacts, revealing the spirit and unspoken assumptions of an era. Often, one vivid image will encapsulate an entire spectrum of attitudes, as does the billboard of Dr. Eckleburg's eyeglasses over the valley of ash heaps at the dump outside New York City. Once visualized in the pages of F. Scott Fitzgerald's, *The Great Gatsby*, the eyes become a quick shorthand reference, a symbol of the wasteland for the reader to absorb, to recall, and along with Eliot, to have "shored against my ruins."

Is the image of George F. Babbitt, Realtor, still this encapsulated shorthand? Even though Lewis predicted accurately in a letter to his publisher (Dec. 17, 1920) that in two years the country would be talking of "Babbittry," is it still a *potent imagent*, (as is Don Quixote, tilting at windmills, impossible dream or not) or has it joined many others, once trippingly on the tongue,—a Pecksniff? a Malaprop?—now smelling of the academic lamp or attic dust? Lewis, in his 1930 Nobel Prize address, himself accused the

From *Critical Essays on Sinclair Lewis*, ed. Martin Bucco. © 1986 by Martin Bucco.

American Literary Establishment of preferring its literature "clear and cold and pure and very dead," and offered Henry Wadsworth Longfellow as a horrible example, from fifty years before, of such embalmed, boring, genteel artistry. Should we now, another half-century later, insert Lewis' name in Longfellow's place? Is Babbittry dead? Geoffrey Moore, an Englishman, writing a few years after Lewis' death, asked if we had outgrown *Babbitt*—had it gone the way of the flivvers, Kitty Hawks, and the unfenced prairies; ... yet hypocrisy, provincialism, prejudice, all forms of materialism, have only changed their clothes (and not just in America). Babbitt: alive, readable? ... or cold, boring, and very dead?

Recently, attempts to interest new readers in Lewis have emphasized his "sociological imagination," his documentation, his early use of concepts and reportorial devices since popularized by David Riesman, C. Wright Mills, and Erving Goffman, among others, such descriptions of behavior as Inner- and Outer-directed, as alienated, or as gamesmanship. Ever since the Lynds, analyzing Muncie, Indiana as *Middletown* (1927, 1936), social scientists have fashioned their prose techniques after ones Lewis had already used, so that now he reads (more so than in 1922) "just like a sociology book." Sophistication about peer-group pressures is much more likely these days, when sociograms of who prefers whom for "best friend" can be charted and interpreted for fifth graders. There are still signs around us today revealing a wasteland of boredom and conformity, and we may be even more willing than readers in 1922 to look for symbolic significance in ordinary behavior, to "read meaning into" surface details of a small incident in daily life.

Do the surface incidents in *Babbitt* (or *Main Street*, 1920) provide enough cues and contexts to relate them to our habitual daily behavior? Are the images in Eliot's *Waste Land* also discernible in Lewis' prose reporting life in the "Unreal City," Zenith? Will observing George F. Babbitt serve as an objective correlative, a tangible image for a feeling, a state of emotion, as Eliot theorized? As readers, are we able to recognize part of ourselves in Babbitt's behavior? Can we simultaneously discern the "state of feeling" Lewis furnished us? A reader can obtain an image of daily life from a Sears Roebuck or Monkey Ward catalog, although the esthetic goal of also deriving a state of feeling from any image may require noticing rhetorical forms of presentation which are somewhat different from those found in most sociology books.

One way of getting at the "state of feeling" evoked by Babbitt is to compare the original impact with the retrospective interpretations after his death. *Babbitt* was read in 1922 partly by young rebels fleeing the bourgeois middle class backgrounds in which they had grown up, venerating H. L.

Mencken, who having coined a label, the *Booboisie*, quite understandably felt in his review of the novel that *Babbitt* was a "social document of a high order." May Sinclair, acknowledging the realistic effects, predicted, however, that "though nobody will recognize himself ... everybody will recognize somebody else." One small phrase in her review is suggestive of our reactions to the book so many years later. "You can smell the ash heaps behind every house." This minor image can evoke a not so minor feeling in anyone who has removed large clinkers and either powdery or wet ash from a coal-fired grate furnace; it evokes a multi-sensual kinesthetic effect—but most of us now have experience only with oil or gas heat.

Lewis may be "... cold, and very dead" for readers today, unless they can enter the social world the novelist very clearly created at the time he wrote. This holds true for any non-contemporary work. If Thackeray mentions a young woman wearing lavender gloves and a yellow scarf with a purple and wine-red shot silk dress or notes that there were fires (fireplaces) in the bedrooms of a house, some awareness of the significance, of the *variation from the norm*, is helpful. Heated bedrooms are not likely to seem luxurious to a reader today. Babbitt's clear-glass bathroom towel-racks set in nickel wall brackets have to be compared to porcelain or wood-dowel racks (the 1922 norm) to feel their "uptodateness."

Literature is not so much a mirror which *reflects* life realistically as it is a prism or lens which *refracts* selected, condensed aspects of thought and feeling. This refraction exaggerates, as does a convex mirror such as a shiny chrome hubcap, and one frequent justification for scholarly labor is the need to give a reader in a later time some sense of the actual knowledge of the world possessed by the readers at the time of original composition or publication—knowing that it is, indeed, an impossible dream to evoke 100% of it. Any work which has staying power transcends these limitations and offers enough internal clues of tone and context to remain intelligible without recourse to guide books or prefatory essays or "bogus" footnotes like Eliot's to *The Waste Land*. But isn't a Baedeker for a foreign city similar to footnotes and explanations? Should one read it before a trip, or carry it along and stop at every street corner, or read it afterwards?

Mark Schorer, summing up his massive 867 page biography of Lewis, emphasizes Lewis' documentation, his creation of Babbitt, showing the "standardization of business culture and the stultification of morals under middle class convention," concluding that as Americans, even today, we can hardly imagine ourselves without drawing upon Lewis' writings as a background. As recently as April 1968, in a CBS TV documentary filmed in Duluth, Minnesota, a Lions Club heard Pat Hingle deliver a speech spoken by Babbitt to a Booster Club in the 1922 novel and reacted favorably to its sentiments. His values live on. D. J. Dooley, on the other hand, feels that it is not documentation, but satiric exaggeration, the shaping by genre and formal technique, by literary convention, which enables the book to affect us, by *intensifying* and *ordering* our experiences, pointing out to us, Baedeker-fashion, what we then perceive. If art historian Ernst Gombrich is right that in viewing a painting "the innocent eye sees nothing," because it is both naive and untutored in what to look for, the same conclusion seems doubly applicable to the reader of such a genre as satire. How do you tell photographic realism from the satirical warping of the shiny hubcap?

Lewis, especially in later life, when he went camping with some Duluth real estate men, gave evidence of liking much of George F. Babbitt as an individual. Some of his readers, in 1922 and later, selected only the details they wished to dislike; and many times over the past several decades, particularly during the booming enrollments of the 1960's, academics in English departments have snorted at poor Babbitt playing with his new toy, an automobile dashboard cigar lighter, while themselves fingering the latest cassette or photocopy gadget and measuring the zip in their department in quantified terms. (They are more likely to recognize Babbittry and Boosterism in an administrator's request for the total number of student credit hours produced in their classes, however.)

Any cluster of literary or cultural conventions can trip up "the innocent eye"; conventions, by their nature, are often common, unobtrusive, accepted as a matter of course, as unspoken agreements by writer and reader, speaker and hearer, agreements "to act as if X were really so," even though both know that it is not true.

When Lewis mentions the German immigrant farm women in Gopher Prairie waiting patiently for their men while sitting in the wagons hitched outside the saloon on Main Street, we can, fifty years later, recognize some shift in the cultural "convention." (Don't kid yourself, though, that all the wives would now be in the bar, too.) Lewis was capable, even as late as 1949, failing in health, two years before his death, of recording significant small changes in the details of daily life, changes in fashion and cultural conventions. On returning from a year in Italy, he noticed that men's clothing was more colorful, that moccasins were worn in public even by elderly men, and that TV was becoming common in bars. In an introduction to David L. Cohn's *The Good Old Days* (1939), a collection of materials from old Sears, Roebuck catalogs, Lewis himself judges the value of reporting "things," the social and material surface of life. He put it this way: "Mankind is always more interested in living than in Lives.... By your eyebrow pencils, your encyclopedias, and your alarm clocks shall ye be known."

There are, in addition to cultural conventions, cues for the reader in the conventions and techniques of humor: dialect, exaggeration, juxtaposition, all embodied in this sample by Finley Peter Dunne, creating the comments of Mr. Dooley, an Irishman in a tavern on Archey Road back of the stockyards in Chicago at the turn of the century—the cultural tradition for Mayor Daley, if you please. Discoursing to the bartender and all the others, Mr. Dooley packs into one sentence many of the shifts of tone which let us know that satire, even with a straight face, is not the same as a tape recorder set next to the draft beer spigot. The subject is the benefits of progress and inventions during the reign of Queen Victoria: "An' th' invintions—th' steam-injine, an' th' printin'-press an' th' cotton-gin an' th' gin sour, an' th' bicycle an' th' flyin' machine an' th' nickel-in-th'-slot machine an' th' Croker machine an' th' sody-fountain an'—crownin' wur-ruk iv our civilization—th' cash ray-gisther." Readers can leap the seventy year barrier here by noting the contrasts and the build-ups: locomotives to one-person wheels, the pun on gin, the latest (airplane experiments) to the less lofty items, including the New York City political machine of Boss Croker, from the productive to the consumptive—sody fountains—and finally to the basis of it all, money. This is not too far a cry from the satirical accumulations of detail in both *Main Street* and *Babbitt*.

Some critics, even in the twenties, perceived Lewis as sharing one traditional frame with Eliot, feeling that both men evoked comparison with Dante's *Inferno*. Such a suggestion for reading a work "places" it, offering a perspective for the innocent eye. Alfred Kazin has suggested that the "sheer terror immanent in the commonplace" makes Lewis' picture of Babbitt's unsuccessful rebellion and return to the values of conformity and boredom more terrifying than some of Faulkner. Lewis was reacting against a romanticizing taste which was either interested only in the distant (long ago or far away) or could treat the commonplace only by glamourizing, falsifying, sentimentalizing or prettifying it. This "literary" tone contrasts with the clichés Babbitt and his cronies use, or with Eliot's colloquial description of Lil in the pub or of Madame Sosostris with her *wicked* pack of cards, drawing ironically on both the older use by non-card playing Methodists and the more contemporary use as a term of approval. Today, furnishing a Baedeker for Babbitt's desert (placing it in the tradition of the dark night of the soul would be a bit much) and sharpening the reader's reactions to the details in texture and surface, the effects of language, may be the most effective helpful guides.

"JUG, JUG" TO DIRTY EARS

One major problem in reading a Lewis novel after fifty years have passed concerns its accessibility. Eliot, for instance, footnoted *The Waste Land* in 1922 to make it a thicker book, and in doing so mentions much which he assumed was out-of-the-way reference: Jessie Weston's *From Ritual to Romance*, Tarot, Fisher-Kings, and allusions to Elizabethan drama. He did *not* footnote (although college undergraduate texts now wisely do so) references to the City of London banking district, paintings, St. Augustine, Hamlet-Ophelia, *The Tempest*, the Bible, or the meaning of the nightingale's cry, "Jug, Jug." Lewis, also, does not explain allusions, mimicry or traditional references that he assumed would be clear. For the reader today, these sounds may well fall on dirty ears, which miss the tone, just as the innocent eye fails to perceive the structure and symbolic shorthand behind the surface "things" in a painting. Isn't a stock response to "Jug, Jug" likely to link it to moonshine whiskey, hillbillies, or maybe a crock? Or, for those more genteel, not in associations to L'il Abner or Daisy Mae in the comics, but possibly to a link with a loaf of bread and a Thou under a tree somewhere?

In *The Waste Land*, a brief sample of the multi-leveled problem is the reference, which Eliot notes only to an Australian Ballad, for "O the moon shone bright / on Mrs. Porter / and on her daughter / They wash their *feet* in soda water." A Romantic American Indian Maiden often sung about in Eliot's youth in St. Louis, Mo. was Pretty Red Wing, and the lyrics of the refrain indicated that the moon shines bright on pretty Red Wing, with a lot of sighing and crying and some dying thrown in. The opening lines, however, use a fairy-tale convention which was soon turned obscenely into an infantry marching song. There once was an Indian maid, who said she wasn't afraid ... the military version (known to American Legionnaires and high school students between the wars) continued "to lie on the grass ..." etc., etc. Old Wives' Tales and such Southern folklorists as William Faulkner have also sensitized readers nowadays to the effects of lying out under the naked moon, like Eula Varner and others in Yoknapatawpha County. Such echoes of old popular songs may fall on deaf or innocent ears now, just as the title of Faulkner's short story "That Evening Sun Go Down" (which includes a reference to St. Louis in the text) may escape any linkage with "St. Louis Blues." Lurking even further under the surface of Eliot's supposed Australian ballad is the question of tone which shows up in the reference to "feet" as a euphemism and to the soda water as a possible douche or VD prophylaxis. Mrs. Porter can be a conventional reference for brothel-keeper. A reader who picks up the ballad associations only, classifying it as a song of former love, may have enough to move through Eliot's mind-set here, but some of the "Jug, Jug," is falling on dirty ears.

When George F. Babbitt, dressing for work in the first few pages of the novel, puts in his pocket a loose leaf address notebook containing many items, including a curious inscription: DSSDMYPDF (an item Lewis uses the whole paragraph to build up to and leaves unexplained), the function of the detail, like the function of the ballad for Eliot, is clear enough from the context without a footnote—it is a motto or a reminder to himself. Does it gain from a gloss? Lewis wrote to his publisher (Dec. 28, 1920) that Babbitt would be a GAN about a TBM, and we have not lost the facility for using abbreviations over the intervening decades. It is psychologically fitting that Babbitt himself do such things and that in this Great American Novel the Tired Business Man may be telling himself "Don't Say Something Dumb-Mouthed You Poor Damn Fool."

Lewis indicated in an interview later published in the *University of Kansas City Review* (1958) by Allen Austin that he had deliberately had Carol Kennicott in *Main Street* decorate a room in bad taste to show that while she was bright, she was not *that* bright. The old golden oak table, brocaded chairs, and family photographs were replaced with a japanese obi hung on the maize wall, sapphire velvet pillows with gold bands, and in keeping with the yellow and blue color scheme, a squat blue jar placed on a square cabinet, between yellow candles. Since Lewis arranged the list in this order, ending climactically with the jar, a reader today might have some contextual cues for the "bad taste" in her decorating.

When Chum Frink (the "poet") tells his fellow Booster Club members that they ought to Capitalize Culture (supporting the symphony orchestra for instance), is the pun for capital as $ and capital as emphasis—big letter C—sufficiently clear? Babbitt's son, Ted, was named for the President in office at his birth, Teddy Roosevelt, a good liberal reform Republican. Even this small detail gives some insight into George F's penchant for conforming to current fashions, for admiring the powerful, and for respecting the Great Institutions of American Life.

Lewis could be blatant in his choice of names or his characteronyms. The evangelist, Billy Sunday, turned ever so slightly into Mike Monday preaching at a revival meeting. Babbitt was first tentatively named George Pumphrey, then Fitch, but whether Lewis intended to evoke all the associations since discovered in the sound of his final name, Babbitt, is unanswerable. Does the name currently suggest any of the following—B. T. Babbitt Household Cleaner (and who remembers Bab-O and Sapolio?); a frictionless metal used in machine tool work (the Realtor in the gears of

Commerce); *babble*, as the talk in the novel goes on and on; or *babyish*, as his details of dreaming at the beginning are added to later in the novel? As with reading a Baedeker *afterward*, these can be fitted into the experience of reading the novel on recalling it, but do they jump out crying "Jug, Jug" on first reading?

When Genevieve Taggard, commenting upon a machine age exhibition of artists in New York, quoted one artist, Louis Lozowick, approvingly from the viewpoint of the *New Masses*, the Marxist magazine she was writing for (July 1927), she used the word "plastic" in a different sense than it is likely to have for many readers now: "The artist must objectify the dominant experience of our epoch in plastic terms that possess value for more than this epoch alone." (Printed in F. J. Hoffman, *The Twenties*, p. 291.) Here "plastic" seems to have favorable connotations of shapable and adaptable, without the negative, imitative, unnatural, unfeeling associations more likely today. Does Lewis, conveying the tedium of the porch swing and the mosquitoes on a hot summer night in Gopher Prairie, or the boredom and ennui of George Babbitt as he moves daily through his "plastic" life—in the recent sense—objectify the emotional experience for the reader so that it now possesses value for us? Just such shifts in the tonal resonance for common words can impede our access to an earlier work, Eliot's, Lewis' or that of any other author.

Lewis' most widely recognized technique, however, is the catalog, probably epitomized in the two views of Dyer's drug store in *Main Street*, when both Carol and Bea Sorenson (a Swedish farm girl just coming into town who becomes the Kennicott hired girl or maid) see greatly different details for the soda fountain. Carol's "electric lamp with the red and green and curdled yellow shade over the greasy marble fountain," becomes Bea's "huge fountain of lovely marble with the biggest shade you ever saw—all different kinds of colored glass stuck together; and the soda spouts they were silver, and they came right out of the bottom of the lamp shade!" In *Babbitt*, this device was augmented by the description of daily rituals, dressing, starting the car, filling the gas tank on the drive downtown, each with its own style of ceremonial behavior and speech. These devices offered readers in the 1920's a fresh way of looking at the routines of life around them, but they were not likely to accept that view as factually accurate, since they could discount exaggeration on the basis of their own experiences. While they might find Veblen's notions of conspicuous consumption should lead them to the conclusions, as Anthony Hilfer puts it, that Babbitt, like his dashboard cigar lighter, was decorative but non-productive, and that many of the real estate subdivisions really were the way Lewis described them, they knew life around them and how people actually spoke. They could recognize the half-truths and mimicry on a different plane of experiential evidence than we do fifty years later, when we must pay more attention to stylistic devices and stock responses in order to recognize Babbitt as a real toad, maybe, but in an imaginary garden. Some readers and critics in the past have reversed this order; Lewis reported parts of a real garden, but created a cardboard toad. In contrast to this, there are still some students, after finishing their reading, who will sigh, "but he sounds just like my father."

The ultimate question, then, for investing time and energy in reading *Babbitt* or about a woman's life in a small town before the automobile changed things, as in *Main Street*, is whether or not the plastic terms, the technique and surface texture of the novels, clear in their own epoch, can transmit to a later time a feeling about values, ennui, a wasteland or a wasted life. Do the details we notice in reading *order* and *intensify* our own experience(s)? Do we experience, and not just cognitively recognize, the stultification, the boredom, the desire for escape, and gain insight into what Lewis (at age 46) writing to his publisher (Dec. 28, 1920) called Babbitt's life of compromises: "He is all of us Americans at 46, prosperous but worried ... wanting—passionately—to seize something more than motorcars and a house *before it's too late.*"

The opening paragraphs of the novel show Babbitt dreaming of a faery child before the alarm goes off in the morning. In the last sentences of the novel, Babbitt, dreaming now while wide awake, tells his son to live life however he wishes, "Go ahead ... The world is yours." The myth that youth will be better off dies hard in this country. But his own motto, in the small loose-leaf notebook in his pocket is not the Rabelaisian motto over the abbey of Theleme (masterfully ironic satiric statement about Calvinistic predestination in itself)—*fais ce que voudras* (Do what you will). The notebook page, impermanently recorded, loose-leaf, as Babbitt's magic motto, his talisman to ward off evil, his rabbit's foot, is DSSDMYPDF. And this is the way the world ends, not with a bang, but a whimper. (Which quotes another tag line that, like Dr. Eckleburg's view of the ashheaps, we often use as a fragment to shore against our ruins.)

It is a whimper of and for the main character and the society in the novel, not necessarily for a great part of the psyche of the reader. What *Babbitt*, as a good read, can become for us now is a fragment shored against the ruins, against our own psychological memories, our own potential half-forgotten dreams, our own responses to the Sears' and Ward's ads in the Sunday paper. To make this possible requires revivifying, recreating some of the era of 1910–1922 and of attitudes toward spiritual wastelands and backyard ashheaps then, and also requires paralleling those ash heaps from our own experiences.

As Eliot's old man epitomizes it in "Gerontion," "Whatever is kept must be adulterated." We cannot help but adulterate what a reader of 1922 might have responded to, and we cannot help but add, with an uninnocent eye, not only our own experiences (plastic and otherwise), but also those conventions, literary frames, traditional references, ("Jug, Jug!"), which enable us to sense the boredom, as well as the pleasures of George F. Babbitt's day in the life.

Some travelers may require a Baedeker before the trip, rather than afterward. Even knowing what to look for may not completely suppress the potential for inattentive boredom. The motivation of nostalgia, particularly for an era prior to one's birth, is a very tricky bit of magic. How does Lewis show us How We Live Today? The best advice before picking up the book is that which Eliot uses to close the first section of *The Waste Land*: Baudelaire's Preface (about ennui) to *Fleurs du Mal*:

> You know him, [boredom], hypocrite lecteur, mon sembable,
> mon frere. [My hypocritical reader, my double (or shadow),
> my brother.]

NOTE

* From *The Twenties: Fiction, Poetry, Drama*, ed. Warren French (Deland, Fla: Everett Edwards Press, 1975), 87–99. Reprinted by permission of the author and editor.

GORE VIDAL

The Romance of Sinclair Lewis

1.

*E*lmer *Gantry. It Can't Happen Here. Babbitt. Main Street. Dodsworth. Arrowsmith.* Sinclair Lewis. The first four references are part of the language; the next two are known to many, while the last name has a certain Trivial Pursuit resonance; yet how many know it is the name of the writer who wrote *Elmer Gantry*, played in the movie by Kirk Douglas—or was it Burt Lancaster?

Sinclair Lewis seems to have dropped out of what remains of world literature. The books are little read today, and he's seldom discussed in his native land outside his home town, Sauk Centre, Minnesota. Although Sauk Centre holds an annual Sinclair Lewis Day, the guide to his home recently admitted, "I've never read *Main Street*.... I've been reading the biographies." Elsewhere, the Associated Press (July 18) tells us, "About forty copies of Lewis's books are on the shelves of the town library. For the most part, that's where they stay."

"I expect to be the most talked-of writer," Lewis boasted before he was. But the great ironist in the sky had other plans for him. In the end, Lewis was not to be talked of at all, but his characters—as types—would soldier on; in fact, more of his inventions have gone into the language than those of any other writer since Dickens. People still say, in quotes as it were, "It can't

From *The New York Review of Books*, October 8, 1992. © 1992 by *The New York Review of Books*.

happen here," meaning fascism, which probably will; hence, the ironic or minatory spin the phrase now gets. In the half century since Sinclair Lewis (one wants to put quotes about his name, too) what writer has come up with a character or phrase like Babbitt or Elmer Gantry that stands for an easily recognized type? There is "Walter Mitty" and Heller's "Catch-22"; and that's that. Of course, much of this has to do with the irrelevance of the novel in an audio-visual age. It is "Murphy Brown" not "Herzog" that registers, if only for the span of a network season. Finally, even if the novel was of interest to the many, its nature has certainly changed since the first half of the century when serious novelists, committed to realism/naturalism, wrote about *subjects* like the hotel business, the sort of thing that only pop novelists go in for nowadays.

That said, it would seem impossible that a mere biographer could effectively eliminate a popular and famous novelist; yet that is exactly what Mark Schorer managed to do in his 867-page biography, *Sinclair Lewis*.[1] Schorer's serene loathing of his subject and all his works is impressive in its purity, but, at the end, one is as weary of Schorer himself as of Lewis. I once asked Schorer, an amiable man who liked to drink almost as much as Lewis did, why he had taken on a subject that he so clearly despised. The long answer was money; the short, too. In this Schorer did *not* resemble Lewis who, as much as he liked every sort of success, had a craving for Art in an *echt*-American way, and a passion for his inventions; also, he believed that somewhere over the rainbow there was a great good place that would prove to be home. As it turned out, he was never at home anywhere; and his restless changes of address take up altogether too many pages in Schorer's survey, as they must have used up too much psychic energy in Lewis's life, where the only constant, aside from frantic writing and frantic drinking, was, as his first wife sadly observed, "romance is never where you are, but where you are going." Since he never stayed put, he never got there. Wives and women came and went; there were hardly any friends left after the end of the great decade of his life, 1920–1930.

In 1920, the unadmired great man of American letters, William Dean Howells, died, and Lewis published *Main Street*; then *Babbitt* (1922); *Arrowsmith* (1925); *Elmer Gantry* (1927); *Dodsworth* (1929). The Nobel Prize followed in 1930. That was the period when the Swedes singled out worthy if not particularly good writers for celebration, much as they now select worthy if not particularly interesting countries or languages for consolation. Although the next twenty-one years of Lewis's life was decline and fall, he never stopped writing; never stopped, indeed: always in motion.

"He was a queer boy, always an outsider, lonely." Thus Schorer begins. Harry Sinclair Lewis was born in 1885 in Sauk Centre, Minnesota, population 2,800. At the same time a couple of dozen significant American writers were also being brought up in similar towns in the Middle West and every last one of them was hell-bent to get out. Lewis's father, a doctor, was able to send him to Yale. Harry or Hal or Red was gargoyle ugly: red-haired, physically ill-coordinated, suffered from acne that was made cancerous by primitive X-ray treatments. He was a born mimic. He had a wide repertory of characters—types—and he was constantly shifting in and out of characters. But where Flaubert had only one act, The Idiot, Lewis had an army of idiots, and once started, he could not shut up. He delighted and bored, often at the same time.

Although Lewis had been born with all the gifts that a satirist needs to set up shop he was, by temperament, a romantic. Early writings were full of medieval fair ladies, gallant knights, lands of awful Poesie where James Branch Cabell was to stake out *his* territory, now quite abandoned. Lewis also had, even by American standards, absolutely no sense of humor. In a charming memoir his first wife, Grace Hegger, noted, "*Main Street* was not a satire until the critics began calling him a satirist, and then seeing himself in that role, is it possible that [his next book] *Babbitt* became true satire?" The question is double-edged. Like Columbus, Lewis had no idea where he had gone, but the trip was fun. He loved his high-toned heroine, Carol Kennicutt, but if others thought her a joke, he was willing to go along with it.

In youth Lewis wrote yards of romantic verse, much of it jocose; yet he had heard Yeats at Yale and was much impressed by the poetry of the early Yeats. Like most born writers, he read everything: Dickens, Scott, Kipling were his first influences. But it was H.G. Wells's *The History of Mr. Polly* that became for him a paradigm for his own first novel. Like most writers, again, he later claimed all sorts of grand literary progenitors, among them Thoreau, but it would appear that he mostly read the popular writers of his time and on the great divide that Philip Rahv was to note—Paleface versus Redskin— Lewis was firmly Redskin; yet, paradoxically, he deeply admired and even tried to imitate those Edith Wharton stories that were being published when he was coming of age, not to mention *The Custom of the Country*, whose Undine Spragg could have easily served time in a Lewis novel.

The literary world before 1914 is now as distant from us as that of Richardson and Fielding. In those days novels and short stories were popular entertainment. They were meant to be read by just about everybody. Numerous magazines published thousands of short stories of every kind, and a busy minor writer could make as good a living as a minor bank president. Writing was simply a trade that, sometimes, mysteriously, proved to be an art. William Dean Howells had balanced commerce and art with such exquisite tact that he was invaluable as editor and friend to both the Paleface Henry James and the Redskin Mark Twain. Howells himself was a very fine novelist. But he lived too long. For the rising generation of the new twentieth century, he was too genteel, too optimistic (they had carelessly misread him); too much Beacon Street not to mention London and Paris and the Russia of Dostoevsky, whose first translations Howells had brought to the attention of those very conventional ladies who were thought to be the principal audience for the novel in America.

While still at Yale, Lewis headed straight to the action. Upton Sinclair had started a sort of commune, Helicon Hall, at Englewood, New Jersey, and in 1906 Lewis spent two months there, firing furnaces and writing. By 1909 he was at Carmel with his classmate William Rose Benét, another professional bookman. Lewis worked on the San Francisco *Bulletin*, and wrote. When Jack London had come to Yale to speak for socialism, Lewis had met him. Although Lewis was to be, briefly, a card-carrying socialist, he was never much interested in politics, but he very much admired the great Redskin writer, and he got to know him at Carmel.

London wrote short stories for a living. Unfortunately, he had trouble thinking up plots. Although Lewis was not yet making a living from short stories, he had thought up a great many plots. So, in 1910, Lewis sold Jack London fourteen short story plots for $70. Two became published short stories; the third the start of a not-to-be-finished novel. Lewis later described London at that time as someone more interested in playing bridge than sea-wolfing. He also described how "Jack picked up James's *The Wings of the Dove* ... and read aloud in a bewildered way.... It was the clash between Main Street and Beacon Street that is eternal in American culture." Well, eternity is a long time in bookchat land.

In 1910 Lewis moved on to Washington, DC, which was to become, more or less, his home base in the United States. Meanwhile he worked for New York publishers as reader, copywriter, salesman. He was also selling fiction to the flagship of commercial publishing, *The Saturday Evening Post*, as well as to other magazines. From 1913–1914 he produced a syndicated book page that was carried in newspapers all around the country. By putting himself at the center of bookchat, he insured good reviews for his own books in much the same way that in England now ambitious young writers not only review each other's books but also often act as literary editors in order to promote their future reviewers. Those destined for greatness will eventually review television programs in a Sunday newspaper, thus getting to know the television and film magnates who will, in due course, promote them personally on television as well as buy their products for dramatization. The English literary scene today is very much like that of the US pre-1914.

Lewis's first novel, *Our Mr. Wrenn*, is very much school of Wells: it was, of course, well-reviewed by his fellow bookmen. In the next four years Lewis published four more novels. Each had a subject, of which the most interesting was early aviation, *The Trail of the Hawk* (1915). Lewis had got to know Paul Beck, one of the first army flyers, and the novel presages, rather eerily, Lindbergh's career. In my memory these books are rather like those of Horatio Alger that I was reading at the same time, something of an agreeable blur. Since the Subject comes before the Characters and since Lewis was a thorough researcher, there are many little facts of the sort that pop writers today provide us as they take us on tours of the cosmetics or munitions businesses, subjects they usually know very little about beyond idle, as opposed to dogged, research. Only James Michener, through hard work, has mastered the fictional narrative as a means of instruction in a subject of interest to him, like Hawaii; and then to millions of others.

The first five novels established Sinclair Lewis as a serious if not particularly brilliant novelist; but one with, as they say at *Billboard*, a bullet. As a careerist, Lewis was an Attila. In his pursuit of blurbs, he took no prisoners. He cultivated famous writers. *Main Street* is dedicated to James Branch Cabell *and* Joseph Hergesheimer, the two classiest novelists of the day. *Babbitt* is dedicated to Edith Wharton, who took it all in her magnificent, ruthless stride.

In 1915 his old mentor Upton Sinclair was invited to assess the product. He did:

> You seem to me one of the most curiously uneven writers I have ever known. You will write pages and pages of interesting stuff, and then you will write a lot of conversation which is just absolute waste, without any point or worth-whileness at all; and you don't seem to know the difference. Everything of yours that I have read is about half and half .... wherever you are writing about the underworld, you are at your best, and when you come up to your own social level or higher, you are no good.

Nicely, Upton Sinclair adds a postscript: "Don't be cross." Writers usually get other writers' numbers rather more quickly than critics ever do. After all, as contemporaries, they have been dealt much the same cards to play with.

By 1929, the apprenticeship of Sinclair Lewis was over. He had married and become the father of a son, Wells, named for H.G., whom he had yet to meet (Lewis was deeply irritated when people thought that *he* had been

named for Upton Sinclair when his father had named him after one Harry
Sinclair, a dentist of the first rank).

The genus of Lewis's ascent can be located in the year 1916 when he
and his wife, Grace, came to stay in Sauk Centre with Dr. Lewis and his wife,
Sinclair's stepmother. In her memoir, Grace Hegger Lewis is very funny
about what must have been a fairly uncomfortable visit. "One morning when
'the curse' was upon me," Grace asked for breakfast on a tray. The Lewises
said no, while Hal, Grace's name for her husband, was "furious. He had
always taken for granted his affection for his parents and their behavior he
had never questioned. But seeing his family through the eyes of New York
and of marriage he was appalled by his father's overbearing rudeness." Grace
suggests that this visit forced Lewis to see his home town in an entirely new
way and shift the point of view from that of a lonely off-beat lawyer, in what
was to be called *The Village Virus*, to that of Carol, a girl from outside the
village who marries the local doctor, Will Kennicutt, and so observes the
scene with big city (in her case Minneapolis) eyes.

Grace reports that Dr. Lewis did apologize; the young couple stayed
on; and the town magnates were brought to their knees when they learned
just how much Lewis had been paid for a two-part serial in the *Woman's
Home Companion* ($1,500). "When he told them that it had taken him two
weeks to write the serial, the banker, dividing so much per diem, was visibly
awed.... The young Lewises were to find that this measuring of talent by
dollars was fairly universal, and Hal was hurt at first by this lack of interest
in the writing itself."

Their later life in Washington sounds agreeable. She tells us how they
would walk to the Chevy Chase Club with the young Dean Achesons and
how Lewis also frequented the Cosmos Club and got to know General Billy
Mitchell, Clarence Darrow, and the scarlet lady of our town, Elinor Wylie—
murmur her name, as indeed people were still doing a few years later when I
was growing up. The Lewises seem not to have known the Achesons' friend,
Grace Zaring Stone, author of *The Bitter Tea of General Yen*, who, when told
by a lady novelist—not Elinor Wylie—that she was writing a novel about
Evil, sighed, "If only I had thought of that!"

Lewis maintained that the idea for a novel whose subject would be a
small midwestern market town came to him in 1905. I should suspect that it
was always there. Village life was the first thing that he had known and,
sooner or later, writers usually deal with their origins. The real-life lawyer
Charles T. Dorion was to be the main character, an idealistic soul, able to see
through the pretenses, the hypocrisies, the ... the ... the absolute boredom of
Sauk Centre (renamed by Lewis Gopher Prairie). But the 1916 homecoming
gave Lewis a new point of view, that of his elegant New York wife, to be

called Carol. Dorion was demoted to supporting cast, as Guy Pollack.

In July 1920, in a Washington heat wave, Sinclair Lewis finished *Main Street*. He gave the book to his friend Alfred Harcourt, who had started a new publishing house to be known, in time, as Harcourt, Brace, in which Lewis had invested some of his own money. In the business of authorship he seldom put a foot wrong.

October 23, 1920, *Main Street* was published and, as one critic put it, "if *Main Street* lives, it will probably be not as a novel but as an incident in American life." Even Schorer, not yet halfway through Lewis's career, concedes, a bit sadly, that the book was "the most sensational event in twentieth-century American publishing history." As of 1922 an estimated two million Americans had read the book; and they went right on reading it for years. With Howells gone, Lewis took his place as numero uno and reigned both at home and abroad until 1930, after which, according to Schorer, "with the increasing conformity at the surface of American life and the increasing fragmentation at its base, there have been no contenders at all." I'm not sure that Bill or Ernest or Scott or Saul or Norman or ... would agree. The contenders are all in place. The problem is that fiction—stories intended to be read by almost everyone—ceased to be of much interest to a public "with no time to read" and movies to go to and, later, television to watch. *The Saturday Evening Post* serial, often well-written by a good writer, would now be done, first, as a miniseries on television or as a theatrical film. Today nonfiction (that is, fictions about actual people) stuffs our magazines and dominates best-seller lists.

In any case, *pace* Schorer, conformity in American life, whatever that means, would certainly be a spur to any writer. As for fragmentation, it is no worse now as the countryside fills up with Hispanics and Asians as it was when Lewis was describing the American hinterland full of Socialist Swedes and comic-dialect Germans. Actually, to read about the career of Sinclair Lewis is to read about what was a golden age for writing and reading; now gone for good.

Lewis's energetic self-promotion among the masters of the day paid off. His dedicatees Cabell and Hergesheimer wrote glowing testimonials. Predictably, the novel appealed to the English realists and not to Bloomsbury. The former wrote him fan letters—John Galsworthy, H.G. Wells, Rebecca West; presently he would be taken up by the monarch of bookchat and the master of the fact-filled realistic novel, Arnold Bennett. At home a fellow Minnesotan wrote him "with the utmost admiration," F. Scott Fitzgerald. But five years later Fitzgerald is wondering if *Arrowsmith* is really any good. "I imagine that mine [*Gatsby*] is infinitely better." Sherwood Anderson leapt on and off the bandwagon. Dreiser ignored the phenomenon but his friend H.L. Mencken was delighted with Lewis, and praised him in *Smart Set*. When Lewis's sometime model Edith Wharton won the Pulitzer Prize for *The Age of Innocence*, Lewis wrote to congratulate her. As for this uncharacteristic lapse on the part of a committee designed to execute, with stern impartiality, Gresham's Law, Mrs. Wharton responded with her usual finely wrought irony: "When I discovered that I was being rewarded by one of our leading Universities—for uplifting American morals, I confess I *did* despair." She praises Lewis vaguely; later, she is to prove to be his shrewdest critic.

While Mr. and Mrs. Sinclair Lewis toured restlessly about Europe, trying to enjoy his success, he was already at work on *Babbitt*.

2.

The Library of America has now brought out both *Main Street* and *Babbitt* in a single volume, and it was with some unease that I stepped into the time-warp that is created when one returns after a half century not only to books that one had once lived in but almost to that place in time and space where one had read the old book—once upon a time in every sense. It was said of Lewis that, as a pre-1914 writer, he had little in common with the rising generation of post-World War writers like Hemingway, Dos Passos, Faulkner. It might equally be said that those of us who grew up in the Thirties and in the Second War made as great a break with what had gone before as today's theoreticians made with us. Literary history is hardly an ascending spiral, one masterpiece giving birth to an even greater one, and so on. Rather there are occasional clusters that occur at odd intervals each isolated from the others by, no doubt, protocreative dust. Lewis was pretty much his own small star lying between Twain, Crane, James, and Wharton, and the small but intense postwar galaxy which still gives forth radio signals from that black hole where all things end. In the Twenties, only Dreiser was plainly Lewis's superior but Dreiser's reputation was always in or under some shadow and even now his greatness is not properly grasped by the few who care about such things.

What strikes one first about *Main Street* is the energy of the writing. There is a Balzacian force to the descriptions of people and places, firmly set in the everyday. The story—well, for a man who supported himself by writing stories for popular magazines and selling plots to Albert Payson Terhune as well as Jack London, there is no plot at all to *Main Street*. Things just happen as they appear to do in life. In Minneapolis, Carol Milford meets Will Kennicutt, a doctor from the small town of Gopher Prairie. There are events, some more dramatic than others, but the main character is Main

Street and the intense descriptions of the place are most effective, while the people themselves tend to be so many competing arias, rendered by a superb mimic usually under control. Later, Lewis would succumb to his voices and become tedious, but in *Main Street* he is master of what Bakhtin (apropos Dostoevsky) called "the polyphonic novel.... There is a plurality of voices inner and outer, and they retain 'their unmergedness.'" Lewis is splendid on the outer voices but he lacks an idiosyncratic inner voice—he is simply a straightforward narrator without much irony—while his attempts to replicate the inner voices of the characters are no different, no more revelatory, than what they themselves say aloud.

"On a hill by the Mississippi where Chippewas camped two generations ago, a girl stood in relief against the cornflower blue of Northern sky." The first sentence is brisk; it places us in time—reminds us that this was Indian territory a half century ago, and so the white man is new to the scene, and his towns are still raw. "Cornflower" is *Saturday Evening Post*. "Corn" itself is a bit dangerous, as in corny. "Blue" isn't all that good either. Yet, paradoxically, Lewis had a lifelong hatred of the cliché in prose as well as a passion for sending up clichés in dialogue: this can cause confusion.

Anyway, he has now begun the story of Carol Milford, enrolled at Blodgett College, a girl full of dreams even more vivid than those of Emma Bovary—dreams rather closer to those of Walter Mitty than to Flaubert's Emma, though, in practice, as it later proves, Carol has more than a touch of Bouvard and Pécuchet in her when she takes to the field with one of her projects to bring beauty to a drab world. Lewis maintained that, as of 1920, he had read neither *Madame Bovary* nor Edgar Lee Master's *Spoon River Anthology*, whose set of arias from the simple dead folk of a small-town cemetery inspired a generation of writers, achieving a peak, as it were, in Thornton Wilder's *Our Town*.

Carol is involved in the "tense stalking of a thing called General Culture." Ostensibly on her behalf, Lewis drops Culture names all over the place. First, Robert G. Ingersoll, the nineteenth-century agnostic, and then Darwin, Voltaire. One can't really imagine her liking any of them—she is too romantic; she dreams of truth and beauty. Ingersoll is a hardbitten, dour free-thinker. The other two are outside her interest. Later he tells us that she has read Balzac and Rabelais. Since she becomes a librarian, the Balzac would be inevitable but neither Carol nor Sinclair Lewis ever read Rabelais. There are some things that an experienced dispenser of bookchat knows without *any* evidence.

At a Minneapolis party, Carol meets Dr. Will Kennicott, a doctor in the small town of Gopher Prairie. He is agreeable, and manly, and adores her. In a short time: "He had grown from a sketched-in stranger to a friend."

Will is "sincere" (a favorite word of Carol's is "insincere"). Carol meanwhile (as a result of Mrs. Wharton on interior decoration and *Italian Gardens*?) has dreamed that "what I'll do after college [is] get my hands on one of those prairie towns and make it beautiful. Be an inspiration. I suppose I'd better become a teacher then.... I'll make 'em put in a village green, and darling cottages, and a quaint Main Street!" Hubris is back in town. One doubts if the worldly Grace Hegger Lewis ever thought along those lines in Sauk Centre in 1916. But Lewis has got himself a nice premise, with vast comic potentialities. But instead of playing it for laughs and making satire, he plays it absolutely straight and so achieved total popularity. Irony.

In 1912 Carol and Will get married. They take the train to Gopher Prairie. It is all very much worse than she expected. But Will exults in town and people. Although Lewis is noted for his voices, the best of the novel is the description of things and the author's observations of the people who dwell among the things.

> The train was entering town. The houses on the outskirts were dusky old red mansions with wooden frills, or gaunt frame shelters like grocery boxes, or new bungalows with concrete foundations, imitating stone. Now the train was passing the elevator, the grim storage-tanks for oil, a creamery, a lumber-yard, a stock-yard muddy and trampled and stinking.

They are met by Will's friends, the elite of the village. There is a lot of kidding. Mock insults. Ho-ho-ho.

> Main Street with its two-story brick shops, its story-and-a-half wooden residences, its muddy expanse from concrete walk to walk, its huddle of Fords and lumber-wagons, was too small to absorb her. The broad, straight, unenticing gashes of the streets let in the grasping prairie on every side. She realized the vastness and emptiness of the land.

This is "home." She is in a panic. She notes "a shop-window delicately rich in error" (this is worthy of Wharton), "vases starting out to imitate tree-trunks but running off into blobs of gilt—an aluminum ash-tray labeled 'Greetings from Gopher Prairie.'" And so she makes her way down Main Street, all eyes, later ears.

Carol entertains the village magnates, only to discover "that conversation did not exist in Gopher Prairie. ... they sat up with gaiety as with a corpse." Nothing stirs them until one says, "'Let's have some stunts, folks.'" The first to be called on is Dave, who gives a "stunt about the Norwegian catching a hen." Meanwhile, "All the guests moved their lips in anticipation of being called on for their own stunts." A stunt was usually an imitation or ethnic joke. One can imagine Lewis's own lips moving as he would prepare to hold captive some party with a monologue in a character not his own. As it turns out, there is conversation in Gopher Prairie—about "personalities," often in the form of lurid gossip, usually sexual. Carol is not happy.

Lewis is good at tracing Carol's ups and mostly downs. She puts on a play. Everything goes wrong. She joins the Library Board to encourage reading, only to find that the librarian believes that their function is not to lend but to preserve books. This, of course, was the ancestor of today's Sauk Centre Library where Lewis's books are preserved but not read. Carol joins the Jolly Seventeen, the fashionable young matrons of the village where bridge is played and personalities dissected. Carol is thought a bit too citified and definitely stuck-up when she tries to talk of General Culture and town improvements. She does her best to fit in but she "had never been able to play the game of friendly rudeness."

In time, Carol flirts with the lawyer, Guy Pollack. He loves literature and disdains the town and one can see that Lewis had it in mind to bring them together but Guy is too damp a character. She drops him; then she goes off in two unexpected directions. A beautiful young Swedish tailor has come to town, Erik Valberg. A townswoman soliloquizes: "They say he tries to make people think he's a poet—carries books around and pretends to read 'em, says he didn't find any intellectual companionship in this town…. And him a Swede tailor! My! and they say he's the most awful mollycoddle—looks just like a girl. The boys call him Elizabeth…." Plainly, the influence of Willa Cather's curiously venomous short story "Paul's Case" of 1905 was still strong enough for Lewis to ring changes on the sissy boy who dreams of art and civilization and beauty.[2]

As it turns out, Erik is not hot for Will but for Carol. They talk about poetry; they lust for each other. They are two against the town. He is randy Marchbanks to her Candida. But nothing happens except that everyone suspects, and talks; and Lewis is at his best when he shows Carol's terror of public opinion in a place where it is not physically possible to escape from eyes at windows. This sense of claustrophobia and of no place to hide is the heart of the book. Even the metaphor of the unending "grasping" prairie contributes to the stifling of the individual.

Erik is a farm boy turned tailor turned autodidact: he has got the point. "It's one of our favorite American myths that broad plains necessarily make broad minds, and high mountains make high purpose. They do just the opposite." Carol's attempts to integrate him in the town fail. Will observes them walking together at night. There is no scene, but it is clear that Erik must leave town, which he does.

The other counterpoint voice to Gopher Prairie is Miles Bjornstam, unfondly known as "the Red Swede." He is a self-educated laborer; he cuts wood, does odd jobs, lives in a shack like Thoreau. He reads Veblen. Reading lists of the characters are all important to Lewis. Carol has not only read but bought "Anatole France, Rolland, Nexe, Wells, Shaw, Edgar Lee Masters, Theodore Dreiser, Sherwood Anderson, Henry Mencken." Of those on this list, three subsequently gave Lewis blurbs. Ambitious pen-persons take note.

Daringly, Carol pays Miles a call; he shocks and delights her by putting into words her own thoughts about the village. Then he goes into business for himself; prospers with a dairy; marries Carol's best friend, her maid-of-all-work, Bea Sorenson, who comes from the hinterland and though she speaks with a comic Scandinavian accent her heart is gold. Earlier, the village was scandalized that Carol had treated her as an equal. Now, although Mr. and Mrs. Bjornstam are hard-working and prosperous, they are still shunned, partly because of their foreignness and low class but mostly because the agnostic Miles has been "lippy" about the greatest nation in the country and the most perfect of its Main Streets. With the arrival of the First World War everyone is now a super-American, busy demonizing all things foreign—like Miles and Bea. But Carol continues to see the Bjornstams and their child. She, too, has a son.

It is during these scenes that Lewis must do a fine balancing act between melodrama and poetic realism in the Hardy vein (sometimes Hardy, too, lost his balance). The Bjornstams are the only people Carol—and the reader—likes. But the villagers continue to hate them even though Miles has done his best to conform to village ways.

Bea and her child get typhoid fever, from the bad water that they must drink because the neighbor with the good water will not share. Will Kennicutt does his best to save Bea and her child but they die. Carol is shattered. Miles is stoic. When the ladies of the village unexpectedly call with gifts, not knowing that mother and child are dead, Miles says, "You're too late. You can't do nothing now. Bea's always kind of hoped that you folks would come see her.... Oh, you ain't worth a God-damning." Like Erik, he, too, leaves town.

Set piece follows set piece. There is a trip to California where Will searches for fellow villagers and, unhappily for Carol, finds them. She is now ready to leave Gopher Prairie, "Oh, is all life, always an unresolved but?" She resolves the "but." She will get out into the world, *any* world but that of the claustrophobic censorious village folk. Will accepts her decision even though he continues to be In Love With Her. (Rather unlikely this.) Carol and son set out for Washington, DC—the city from which we locals used to set out for New York as soon as we could. On the train east, the boy asks where they are going and Carol says, "We're going to find elephants with golden howdahs from which peep young maharanees with necklaces of rubies, and a dawn sea colored like the breast of a dove ..." John Cheever would, years later, redo this bit of purple most tastefully.

The elephants turn out to be the Bureau of War Risk Insurance, where she does clerical work, and in mythical, magical Washington "she felt that she was no longer one-half of a marriage but the whole of a human being." She moves among army, navy, minor officialdom. She revels in "the elm valley of Massachusetts Avenue ... the marble houses on New Hampshire Avenue ..." and the splendors of the restaurant on the roof of the Powhatan Hotel.

Will pays her a call; she is now a whole woman and so able to return to Gopher Prairie; she is, somehow, mysteriously, at peace with its boredom and mean-spiritedness. But she will not be coopted; she will not be a booster. She has another child. She sees Erik again—at the movies, up there on the silver screen; he had found his way to Hollywood. "I may not have fought the good fight," Carol says at the end to Will, "but I have kept the faith." On those words of William Jennings Bryan, the book ends.

3.

Babbitt was intended to be the account of a single day in the life of the eponymous protagonist, a realtor in the great city of Zenith, an extension and enlargement of Gopher Prairie, with elements of sultry Duluth where the Lewises had lived for a season and were—what else?—the cynosure of all eyes. The day that Lewis had picked was one in April 1920, and we follow George F. Babbitt from the moment that he awakens with, significantly, a hangover to the end of the day, but by that time Lewis had decided that one day wasn't going to be enough for him to do his stunts in, so the story continues another year or two, and a Mid-western Bloom was not to be.

Lewis's eye for detail is, as always, precise. We get an inventory of bathroom and house and sleeping porch, a fad of the day that I have just recalled with the sense of having slipped several notches back in time. There is a long-suffering wife, a son, two daughters—one at Bryn Mawr. Babbitt is forty-six years old. Prohibition has been in place for a year, so everyone drinks too much. There is talk of the coming election, and the great shadow of Warren Gamaliel Harding is already darkening the land and his famous injunction, "Don't knock, boost," is on every Zenith businessman's lip.

Babbitt himself is vaguely unhappy; "the Babbitt house," apparently, "was not a home." But all the latest gadgets are on display. There is chintz, but no heart. The real estate business is booming.

Even so, he dreams of "a fairy child," a recurring dream that somehow underscores Lewis's uneasiness with sex, mature or otherwise. Babbitt has been true to his wife, Myra, since he married her, something that is hard for us plague-ridden *fin-de-siècle* types to fathom. As a result, he lusts for other women in his heart and, sooner or later, lust must be served. This gives the story what small impetus it has: How—and for whom—will he fall, and what kind of mess will he make?

As in *Main Street* there is no plot, only set scenes. Lewis notes the class divisions. There is the class above Babbitt that belongs to the Union Club as best emblemized by Charles McKelvey; then there is the Athletic Club where Babbitt and his fellow boosters hang out and denounce socialism and labor unions and anarchists. Meanwhile, at the wheel of his new car, a "perilous excursion," Babbitt daydreams enroute to his office, the "pirate ship." He has had his first conversation of the day with a neighbor, and they have talked of the weather in great detail and though their exchange should be as tedious as the real thing, Lewis is a master of those grace notes of boring speech that put one in mind of Bach. "There was still snow at Tiflis, Montana, yesterday," said the neighboring Bore; then goes for a crescendo: "Two years ago we had a snow-squall right here in Zenith on the twenty-fifth of April."

Next, a loving description of Zenith—skyscrapers now—and old houses, movie billboards, drugstores, factory suburbs, a proper city where once the Chippewas roamed. At the office there is a young partner, a secretary—Babbitt's father-in-law is senior partner, and seldom seen. Babbitt is having what now would be called a midlife crisis of a sexual nature: "In twenty-three years of married life he had peered uneasily at every graceful ankle, every soft shoulder; in thought he had treasured them; but not once had he hazarded respectability by adventuring." Plainly, Lewis is not drawing on autobiography. Although he preferred drink to sex, he had, at least once, in Italy, cheated on Grace, and one does not suppose him to have been pure premarriage. What is interesting about Lewis's description of Babbitt's sex life is whether he is distorting it deliberately to give American readers, a high-toned, censorious, prudish lot, a picture of an average American businessman, true as steel to the little lady, or whether he has some arcane knowledge of how Zenith males denied themselves. It is hard to know what to think. Even in the Gopher Prairie of Springfield, Illinois, in the 1840s there were girls to be rented by young lawyers like A. Lincoln and J. Speed. Yet in 1920 Babbitt has only masturbatory images, and the recurring mawkish dream of the "fairy girl."

Babbitt has only one actual friend, even though he himself is a prototypical gregarious regular fellow and very well liked. But he had been at a school with Paul Riesling, who had wanted to be a musician; instead Paul married a virago (whom he will later shoot but not, alas, kill—he does serve time). Paul and Babbitt revert to adolescence when together. They romanticize their common past. Babbitt was to have been a powerful tribune of the common man and Paul a world-class violinist. But since neither is articulate, when they are together they can only tell jokes, as they try, rather wistfully, to go back in time to where they had been, if nothing else, real. They dream now of going off together on a hunting trip.

Babbitt has lunch at the Athletic Club. Lewis delights in reproducing the banalities of the Joshers, Good Fellows, Regular Guys. Kidding, chaffing, "stunts"—all these pass for communication and the fact that Lewis could reproduce this sort of conversational filler delighted those who went in for it, which was most Americans, while British book reviewers acknowledged that Lewis's Joshers confirmed their worst fears about the collective cretinism of the separated cousinage. I cannot think how the French took Lewis's dialogue in translation. Bouvard and Pécuchet are like figures from Racine when compared with the Boosters of the Athletic Club. In any case, Lewis had somehow struck a universal class nerve and, for a time, everyone was delighted by his hyper-realism. Even so, Edith Wharton struck a warning note. She was, she wrote, duly grateful for the dedication to herself of *Babbitt* but she saw fit to make one suggestion: "In your next book, you should use slang in dialogue more sparingly. I believe the real art in this respect is to use just enough to *colour* your dialogue, not so much that in a few years it will be almost incomprehensible." She admired his "irony," wondering how much of it Americans got.

I suspect they got none; the book was taken as just like life and Lewis was hardly more critical of Americans and their values than his readers were. They, too, hankered after fairy girls in dreamland as well as magic casements elsewhere, preferably in Europe, through which they might, like Alice, step into Wonderland. The secret of Lewis and his public was that he was as one with them. Grace thought that the crown of ironist he had been mistakenly awarded by those who read *Main Street* obliged him to go for the real diadem in *Babbitt*. But I think he just kept on recording.

The story proceeds with random events. Babbitt becomes an orator for the realtors; he takes part in the election of a Republican mayor; tries to move up socially and fails; he drinks more and more, the most vivid description in the book is the way booze was sold clandestinely at an ex-saloon, a sordid place, "giving that impression of forming a large crowd which two men always give in a saloon."

Lewis makes an odd obeisance to Howells, whom he will dismiss, so foolishly, at the Nobel Prize ceremony of 1930. Lewis calls the state capital Galop de Vache, in memoriam of the hometown of the journalist-hero of that Florentine tale *Indian Summer*, who hailed from Des Vaches, Indiana.

Babbitt is essentially a *roman fleuve* despite its snappy scenes and bright "stunts." In due course, the river deposits Babbitt on the not-so-wild shore of love. He meets a demimondaine lady of a certain age, Mrs. Tanis Judique. She is arty; she has a salon of marginal types. Tactfully, Myra Babbitt has retreated, temporarily, to her family and so Babbitt is able to conduct his love affair in relative peace while drinking more and more in the company of the feckless young. Business is affected: deals are lost. He falls in with the town radical, Seneca Doan, another variation on the original Dorion, with a bit of Upton Sinclair thrown in. Doan has been defeated for mayor. He now supports a local strike. Babbitt falls under his spell for a time (they had known each other in college). Then the town turns on Babbitt. Adultery does not disturb the boosters so much as Babbitt's timid support of the strikers. In a series of confrontations almost as terrible as the one at the end of *The Age of Innocence* Zenith threatens to destroy him; and Babbitt caves in. He has not fought the good fight, and he has not kept much of any faith to anything but, at the end, he will "'start something': he vowed, and he tried to make it valiant." Meanwhile, happy ending. Tanis and Seneca slink away; wife comes home. Valiant.

March 26, 1925, Lewis wrote his publisher, "Any thoughts on pulling wires for [*Arrowsmith*] for Nobel Prize?" There were such thoughts, there were such wires. By 1930 the Swedes were at last ready to pick an American. Earlier, Henry James had been airily dismissed in favor of Maurice Maeterlinck, the Belgian bee-master. The choice was now between Dreiser and Lewis and, as these things are ordered in the land of the great white night, Lewis was inevitably chosen. Mark Schorer writes of all this with distinct sadness. Even the President of the United States, a New England wit called Calvin Coolidge, broke his usual silence—he was a school of Buster Keaton comic—to declare, "No necessity exists for becoming excited."

Lewis lived for twenty-one more years. He produced a great amount of work. He turned to the theater; even acted on stage. He married the splendid journalist Dorothy Thompson, who never stopped talking either. They opposed America's entry onto World War Two, a war in which his son Wells was killed. It is painful to read of Lewis's last days as recorded by Schorer. Drink had estranged him from most people; and so he was obliged to hire young secretaries to play chess with him and keep him company; among those paid companions were the writers-to-be Barnaby Conrad and John Hersey, who has prepared the exemplary Library of America *Sinclair Lewis*.

Mr. Schorer, enraged to the end, notes, finally, "He was one of the worst writers in modern American literature, but without his writing one cannot imagine modern American literature. That is because, without his writing, we can hardly imagine ourselves." This is not a left-handed compliment so much as a rabbit-punch. Whatever Lewis's faults as a writer he never knowingly wrote a bad book or, indeed, one on any subject that he could not at least identify with in imagination. Curiously enough, his ex-wife, Grace Hegger, is more generous (and writes rather better prose) than the biographer:

> Even though Lewis's first successful novels can be recognized as written by him, it is significant that he created no school of writing as have Hemingway and Faulkner, Henry James and Flaubert. He influenced public thinking rather than public writing.

Surely, that is something. As for the man, after his ashes were returned to Sauk Centre, she writes, "Dear, dear Minnesota Tumbleweed, driven by the winds of your own blowing, rootless to the day when your ashes were returned to the soil which had never received your living roots, I offer you these memories. With love from Gracie."

NOTES

1. *Sinclair Lewis: An American Life* (McGraw-Hill, 1961).

2. For a brilliant analysis of Cather's sexual and social confusions read Claude J. Summer's *Gay Fictions* (Continuum, 1980): he believes that in "Paul's Case" Cather was reacting fiercely against the aestheticism of Oscar Wilde (condemned ten years earlier); for her, the young Paul is a Wilde *in ovo*, and doomed. She herself liked men to be men, and women to be men, too. She seemed unaware of the paradox.

JAMES M. HUTCHISSON

"All of Us Americans at 46": The Making of Sinclair Lewis' Babbitt

W hen Sinclair Lewis Published *Babbitt* in 1922, he created an archetypal figure that has since remained in America's cultural consciousness—the standardized middle-class businessman carried along by the tide of consumer culture and boosterism. Lewis also coined a term for this way of thinking which remains in the vernacular today. The process by which he wrote the novel, a topic that has never been examined, is fascinating: among Lewis' papers at The Beinecke Rare Book and Manuscript Library of Yale University there is a wealth of documentary evidence which shows that Lewis systematically and meticulously researched the field of real estate; visited cities to use as possible models for Zenith; and compiled intricately detailed biographies of the leading characters. He even drew maps of the interior and exterior settings in the novel, then wrote a scene-by-scene summary of the plot—all before writing a word of the first draft.

None of these materials has been published previously, or even commented upon in any detail.[1] They provide revealing evidence of the ways in which Lewis conceived, then progressively revised *Babbitt* at three stages: first, there is a series of copious notes on various aspects of 1920s American life and on characters, places, and professions which Lewis used either directly or indirectly in the novel; next, there is a fragment of a rejected outline for an early chapter of the novel which shows that Lewis made

From *The Journal of Modern Literature* 18, no. 1 (Winter 1992). © 1994 Temple University.

significant changes in the structure and focus of *Babbitt* after he had conceived it; finally, there is a completed draft typescript which is a spider's web of blue, red, black, and green pencil markings, but which when unravelled reveals that Lewis made two types of major changes in the characterization of Babbitt. In some portions of the typescript, Lewis tempered his exaggerated portrait, making Babbitt less stereotyped and more realistic. But elsewhere Lewis made many more cuts, sometimes of a dozen or more pages in length, that reduced drastically the human qualities of his character and therefore showed Babbitt in a less sympathetic light, making him more of a type than an individual.

The surviving physical evidence, together with Lewis' almost daily correspondence with his friends and publishers, reveals that Lewis worried over and worked on a series of aesthetic problems as he moved from notes to plan to rough draft, problems which account for some persisting difficulties with interpretations of the novel. In writing Babbitt, Lewis was walking a hairline, trying to balance prose that would communicate both straightforward narrative and satire, trying to write a novel that was a study both of a single character and of that character's milieu, and trying to create a protagonist who was both a type and a multi-dimensional individual. As Lewis told his publisher Alfred Harcourt, he wanted Babbitt to be the "typical T. B. M. [tired business man]," but also a character who would represent "all of us Americans at 46, prosperous but worried, wanting—passionately—to seize something more than motor cars and a house *before it's too late*." The character would be "big in his real-ness ... not in the least exceptional, yet dramatic, passionate, struggling."[2]

*   *   *   *

Glimpses of the figure who would become Babbitt can be seen in parts of *Main Street*—in Percy Bresnahan, who is proud to be a "red-blooded Regular Fellow"; or in "Honest" Jim Blausser, who starts Gopher Prairie on a boosting campaign—and Lewis began planning his "next great realistic novel" while he was still correcting proofs of *Main Street*. From the Maine resort town of Lake Kennebago, Lewis tentatively reported to Harcourt in the late summer of 1920 that his next work would tell "the story of the man in the Pullman smoker, of our American ruler" and its central character would be one "G. T. Pumphrey of Monarch City." Lewis' general conception of his central character remained the same through the fall, when he moved to Washington, D.C., and began work on the novel, but the character's name and the title of the novel, which Lewis had decided should be the same, changed almost weekly. "Pumphrey" was discarded because it was "too English and mite be thought humorous"; "Burgess" Harcourt disapproved of as "too freakish." Both Lewis and Harcourt agreed, however, that the "title name" should not be "too common—like Jones, Smith, Robertson, Thompson, Brown, Johnson—for the reason that then people will associate the name not with the novel but with their numerous acquaintances who have that common name." By the end of November Lewis settled on something entirely different—"Fitch."[3]

Lewis retained the name "Fitch" through the middle of December, as he began his research for the novel, compiling in the process a 193-page notebook. As Harcourt recalled, Lewis put "as much study into the subject matter as a graduate student preparing a Ph.D. thesis."[4] The notebook preserves fascinating documentary evidence of a writer at work—gathering data, filtering it through his imagination, then transforming it into fiction. In conceiving his Balzacian world of Zenith, Lewis provided full supporting details and documented it all on paper before writing the draft typescript. To cite only a fraction of the contents of the notebook: there are entries for "City Institutions"; "Largest Industrial Corporations"; businesses located "On the Ground Floors of Office Buildings"; "Lines of Industry"; "City Song"; and "Kinds of Houses in Floral Heights." For the leading characters Lewis wrote "biographies" varying in length from one paragraph to three pages. For Babbitt, Lewis constructed a genealogy, listed what courses he would have taken in college (by reading the 1889–90 University of Michigan catalog), how he met his wife Myra, when they were married, and so on—a complete past, which Lewis ultimately decided not to use but which is relevant to the changes he made in the characterization of Babbitt. The notebook also contains biographical data on "characters" who do not appear in the novel but whom Lewis created as citizens of his mythic city: "Members of the Boosters' Club"; "Members of the Union Club"; "Staff of Babbitt–Thompson Realty Co."; "Babbitt's Competitors—Realtors and His Allies" (each of whose specialty is identified by abbreviations such as "BU" for business properties and "RM" for farm land); "Neighbors of Babbitt who are not Close Friends"—an entire society of fictional characters.

The copious detail of the notebook also suggests that in planning *Babbitt*, Lewis was planning a series of interrelated novels. There is specific evidence that he was thinking ahead to *Dodsworth* (1929), for he included a page listing "Important Early Families with Descendants in Zenith Today"; at the top of this chart is the name "Dodsworth." Although no information is given about the family, there are other references to the Dodsworths: the Dodsworth Theatre is listed under "City Institutions" and under "Largest Industrial Corps. in Zenith" is listed the "McKelvey and Dodsworth Construction Company," with one Putnam Dodsworth as "third v.p." On two other pages, Lewis worked out a separate genealogy for characters whom he called "Great Souls," in which we again see the names Dodsworth and also Lucile McKelvey, who appears in *Babbitt* and is mentioned in *Dodsworth*. As he wrote *Babbitt*, Lewis was also planning at least one other novel, which would concern the anti-Babbitts, or "great souls." According to this entry, they "scarce enter in the life, and book, of Babbitt, who, when he encounters them, is puzzled; who speaks ill of them; who does not know how lively and fine a social group most of them constitute." And there are scores of other characters in the notebook who never made it past the planning stages, although Lewis used some of them in later novels. For example, "Benoni Carr," whom Lewis intended to be the "New Thought preacher" in *Babbitt*, was reincarnated as the sham medical "professor" in *Arrowsmith* (1925). And "Tub Pearson" is listed among the "grads Eastern c[olle]ges and prep schools ... much at country clubs"; this character appears in *Dodsworth*. Throughout the fall of 1920, Lewis worked out the demographics of his setting and added material to his notebook. By 17 December, he had finished his preliminary research for the novel, settled on "Babbitt" as the name for the title character, and prophetically told Harcourt that "two years from now we'll have them talking of Babbittry...."[5]

The concept of Zenith had begun to take shape, but it lacked verisimilitude. For these details, Lewis went to the Midwest and gathered data first-hand on his subject. He went about his task almost like an anthropologist, mingling with the type of people the novel would concern and making notes on what he observed. During February, March, and most of April 1921, Lewis visited several cities in Illinois, Wisconsin, and Michigan, but he spent most of his time in Cincinnati: "Bully time," he wrote Harcourt, "met lots of people, really getting the feeling of life here. Fine for Babbitt."[6] Study of the material he gathered here shows Lewis incorporating his research directly into *Babbitt*. Clippings from Cincinnati newspapers provided much material. Beside one article listing city districts which would be affected by road construction, among them "Dorchester" and "Silver Grove," the names of two districts in which Babbitt holds rental properties (p. 37), Lewis wrote: "models for names of city suburbs, streets, etc." Once he obtained the raw data, Lewis embellished it and wrote a note outlining how he would use the material in the novel—in this case, Lewis wanted to give a "Picture of, and [do] justice to, all the city" as "a cosmos," mentioning the "excellence of the suburbs in which U.S. equals the world" but also the fact that businessmen do not appreciate the "fine system of parks, symphony orchestra, etc." Lewis also clipped society columns, then replicated their syntax and language in such places as chapter 2, in which Babbitt reads in the Zenith *Advocate–Times* about a dinner given by the McKelveys (pp. 21–2).

Underneath one such clipping Lewis wrote, "By Elnora Pearl Bates," whom he identified in the notebook as the society reporter for the Zenith paper and who appears as such in *Babbitt*.

Objects of satire in the novel came from various quarters. The idea for Babbitt's being forced by his wife to attend a meeting of the "Higher Illumination League" of "The International New Thought Alliance," for instance, derived from an announcement of just such an organization. The similarity of the information in the notebook and the details in the novel is close. In the novel, the speaker is Mrs. Opal Emerson Mudge, who talks on "Cultivating the Sun Spirit" (p. 355), but she might just as well be the speaker noted on the bulletin, "Miss Leona Hale Feathers," who offers an "Advanced Truth Class."

Perhaps the most detailed—certainly the most technical—material in the notebook concerns real estate. Various entries list such items as the cost of "One apartment house in Cincinnati in 1920, with 32 apartments, four stories high." On the back of one page are handwritten calculations which estimate the operating expenses for a firm such as Babbitt's. There is also a description of a real estate office that Lewis visited in Wilmette, Illinois, which he seems to have used as the model for Babbitt's office. It is located on the "Ground floor of bldg containing on same hall a florist and W[estern]. U[nion]. office," and has a "Platform at window" with "pictures of houses, ad of smart cemetery" (*Cf.* p. 34). Stanley Graff's telephone conversation with a prospective client in that same chapter is, but for a word or two, a verbatim transcription of Lewis' note, "Heard over phone here, 'I think I've got just the house that would suit you. Oh, you've seen it. Well, how'd it strike you? Oh, I see'" (*Cf.* p. 33).

Finally, one section of the notebook reveals Lewis perfecting one of his major talents, his ear for mimicking American speech. In this section, "Locutions," Lewis listed whole catalogues of expressions and variations on them: "How's the old Bolsheviki/ anarchist/ grouch today?" Or, "If (—) happens, my name is pants/ I'm a gone goose/ my goose is cooked." Some notes are less precise, but no less methodical—such as "at least as a connective." Lewis even marked some entries as "used" after he had incorporated them into *Babbitt*, among them Babbitt's parting words to Paul at the end of chapter 5: "Don't take any wooden money" (p. 67), or the Reverend John Jennison Drew's description of the church choir as providing "mountains of melody, mountains of mirth" (p. 246), phrases that Lewis jotted down on the bulletin of the First Congregational Church of Oak Park, Illinois, where he evidently attended services on 20 March 1921.

The notebook, in sum, reveals Lewis' extremely strong concern with verisimilitude in *Babbitt*. Yet it also may account for a frequent criticism of the novel, that in it Lewis seems more interested in the socio-historical detail of his subject matter than in the psychological complexities of his characters. Lewis' biographer Mark Schorer commented that "in some ways *Babbitt* is hardly a novel at all" but rather "a highly conscious, indeed systematic series, of set pieces, each with its own topic...."[7] The documentation in the notebook may suggest that Lewis was something of a slave to his research and therefore unable to allow the characters, plot, and theme to evolve freely. This may also account in part for the episodic nature and relative thinness of the plot, as compared to the more unified and substantive narratives in *Main Street* and *Arrowsmith*. Most important, it may provide a reason for the lack of development in Babbitt's character, a problem which many readers, among them Edith Wharton, have noticed: "I don't think 'Babbitt' as good a novel, in the all-around sense, as 'Main Street,' " she told Lewis, "because in the latter you produce a sense of unity & of depth by reflecting Main Street in the consciousness of a woman who suffered from it because she had points of comparison, & was detached enough to situate it in the universe—whereas Babbitt is in & of Zenith up to his chin & over."[8] Indeed, evidence in the "Babbitt Plan" and the draft typescript indicates that Lewis had trouble keeping his focus on the central character and not letting his descriptions of Zenith (or of other characters) detract from the emphasis on Babbitt.

*   *   *   *

In late April 1921, Lewis returned to New York, reported to Harcourt on the successful results of his "interviewing" trip, then sailed for England with his wife Grace in early May. When the Lewises arrived there later that month, they rented a country house in the "tiny old village of Bearsted, near Maidstone, in the heart of Kent farming country" and soon Lewis began "to feel that itch which means that I want to get back to writing." On 12 July, he enthusiastically announced to Harcourt that "He's started—*Babbitt*—and I think he's going to be a corker"; but although Lewis had been "writing a little," his work to this point had consisted mostly of "turning notes into a final plan."[9] The "Babbitt Plan," as it is entitled, was evidently written with reference to material in the notebook, and it differs significantly from the published text, revealing, among other things, that Lewis restructured at least part of the novel, removing much material that pertained to the city of Zenith. More important, he altered to some degree the characterization of Babbitt.[10]

According to the draft typescript, Lewis intended chapter I to be Babbitt's speech before the Zenith Real Estate Board, the famous panegyric to "Our Ideal Citizen." Possibly at Harcourt's suggestion, Lewis revised that chapter before the novel was published and relocated it as part of chapter 14.[11] The four extant pages of the plan headed "CHAPTER II" suggest that Babbitt's dream of the fairy-girl, with which the published novel begins, was originally intended as the second chapter; it was to "end with him dreaming again." In Babbitt's dream, Lewis planned to give a kaleidoscopic picture of the past, describing the founding of Zenith and tracing changes in the appearance of the city by 1885, "quoting" from Mrs. Trollope's account of travel in the United States at that time for a description to use for "Zenith in her day" and borrowing from other sources, such as the commentary about America found in the letters of the English historian James Bryce.

Most of the details for this outline Lewis drew from his notebook. Two pages on the "History of Zenith" contain a strikingly detailed account of its earliest exploration through its founding in 1792, when the city fathers "agreed to and signed a Solemn Covenant." The city was to have been named "Covenant," but "12 years afterward," in 1804, one Peter Dodsworth "had [the] name changed to Zenith, as better for business, i.e. for righteousness." Thus the founding fathers' visions of a "city of beauty and justice" (dubious even then, for Lewis noted parenthetically that these visions were "Dimly ... defined" and "to be aristocratically controlled") quickly became the monument to materialism and rule by wealth that is the Zenith of the novel (plan, p. 12). In creating Zenith, then, Lewis invented for it an entire history that would explain its character in modern times. Yet he elected not to use most of this material and in the typescript made similar cuts that removed "historical" matter.[12] This material, together with the abundant sociological data in the notebook, suggests that at this point Lewis seems to have been planning a novel as much about an environment as about a character. In a letter to H. L. Mencken at about this time, Lewis said that the inspiration for *Babbitt* came from Mencken's review of *Main Street*, which suggested that "what ought to be taken up now is the American city—not NY or Chi but the cities of 200,000 to 500,000—the Baltimores and Omahas and Buffaloes and Birminghams, etc." Lewis also noted that he had "tried like hell" to keep the book from being "altogether satire" on "the boob Babbitt" and focus to an equal degree on "the Rotary Club, ... the Chamber of Commerce, the new bungalows"—that is, on the "forward-looking" American city.[13] Yet Lewis' intentions in this regard shifted, and he made other cuts in the typescript in order to focus the novel on Babbitt instead of Zenith.[14]

Lewis thought through Babbitt's past carefully. Originally Lewis intended to show that in his youth Babbitt was an idealistic dreamer, and he meant to explore the ways in which he had changed. The next part of Babbitt's dream in the rejected plan for chapter 2 shows him as a college student with several characters who later become his friends: Paul Riesling, Irving Tate, Max Kruger, Charley McKelvey, and Seneca Doane. Page two, entitled "IDYLLIC 1890," describes a planned scene "Before D[oane]'s graduation," in which Tate would make an "earnest prophecy" that "Bab [would] become [a] great reform mayor; "Riesling [a] great composer (Wagner still hum)"; "McKelvey [a] millionaire banker"; and "Your humble scribe (Tate) [a] poor G[ree]k prof." Lewis then wrote a parallel list, showing how these characters changed in the subsequent twenty years: "Became— Bab as we see him"; "Riesling in roofing occas. playing cello"; "McKelvey did become millionaire, as contracting builder AND Tate also (see note book)." The rest of the plan follows Babbitt at different points in his life. At age twenty, we see him in college, making his own prophecy:

> I tell you, a fellow hadn't ought to just loaf through life. He ought to have some ideals—like Prof. Udell says. He ought to support good honest political candidates and keep up good reading. He ought—I tell you a fellow ought to take part in all these movements, and make the world better. He hadn't ought to be a hog and just live for himself. (plan, p. 13)

In the novel, of course, Babbitt's idea of a "good honest political candidate" is Lucas Prout, the "mattress manufacturer with a perfect record for sanity" (p. 176), and his idea of "a good story" is not Conrad's *Rescue* but something which "would enable a fellow to forget his troubles" (p. 271). On a later page of the plan, a young Paul Riesling suggests that Babbitt "take a whirl at politics," a possibility which Babbitt ironically rejects out of hand: "Hunka! I've seen enough of politics to know they're dirty, and I want to keep out of them" (p. 15). Other material describes Babbitt's "first big ambitions ... nev[er] realized" and his desire to "pull off something—anything—before it's too late" (plan, p. 13). Lewis also outlined several scenes that described Babbitt's interest in law school and his early disdain for real estate, then paralleled them with Paul Riesling's similarly lofty ambitions (plan, pp. 13–14).

Throughout this plan, we see the irony of Babbitt's transformation from someone who dreamed of idylls in his youth to someone enamored of electric cigar-lighters and gleaming porcelain bathrooms in middle age; but little sense of that emerges in the published novel. Lewis mentions that in college Babbitt was a liberal, but we do not see how he changed. As Sheldon Grebstein has noted, "Surely it is hard for us to believe he could ever have been a wild and dangerous dreamer."[15] In the plan we also see Babbitt in a somewhat more sympathetic light, the light in which his creator seems originally to have seen him. *Babbitt* has always been read as an assault on the American middle class, but this early plan for the novel indicates that Lewis originally intended to show more understanding toward his creation. The perceived lack of sympathy which Lewis had for his characters has been a mainstay of Lewis criticism ever since 1922, when Carl Van Doren claimed in his "Revolt of the Village" essays, that because Lewis railed at dullness and because he equated dullness with stupidity, he seemed to be condescending to his characters, people of shallow intellectual depth.[16] Babbitt's human qualities, then, were somewhat reduced by Lewis' rejection of this plan, and as he revised the typescript, Lewis continued to streamline the novel in ways that Mencken applauded when he reviewed it: "no plot whatever, and very little of the hocus-pocus commonly called development of character."[17]

*   *   *   *

Through July and early August 1921, Lewis was "Babbitting away furiously," finishing his plans for the novel and supplementing them with additional research. He had Grace ask Harcourt to send him books on house plans, "big and little ..., Georgian, Dutch Colonial, and other suburban kinds," which Lewis needed for the "real estate developments in the new novel," especially the many "technical terms." Lewis also read "pompous pamphlets ... which big N.Y. advertising agencies get out telling in phrases of pseudo psychology about their magnificent service," mining them for their "high-falutin 'psychology.'" In addition, he consulted realtors' publications, searching out "not only records of mortgages etc. but also real estate gossip and tips."[18] While in England, Lewis customarily worked "all morning and an hour or so in the afternoon," then went for a "walk or drive or swim" with Grace, "all the time talking Babbitt." At this point Lewis also drew what Grace called "the most astonishingly complete series of maps of Zenith," including "the plans of and furnishing[s of] Babbitt's house ... so that the city, the suburbs, the state" would all be "clear in Hal's mind."[19] These eighteen drawings show the precision with which Lewis fixed his setting and provide further evidence that *Babbitt* was to be the prototype for a series of interrelated novels. One map, for instance, depicts "The State in Which is Zenith," a state that went unnamed until *Arrowsmith*, in which Lewis identified it as Winnemac. A street diagram, "Zenith—Most Important Part," notes where the Babbitts, apparently as a class or level of society, live and also shows the site of the Kennepoose Canoe Club, which figures in *Dodsworth*.[20]

By 3 August 1921, Lewis had written "a little of the actual text" of the novel and thought that "both it and the plan" seemed "corking."[21] He worked steadily on the typescript through the early fall of 1921, then in October left England for Pallanza, Italy, where he took a two and a half-week "lay-off," which Lewis thought had been good for the novel, "not only because of the change but also because I've thought out some good things about it during the period—made those valuable readjustments in the general plan which one doesn't always make if he keeps too close to it for too long."[22] (These "readjustments" included, probably among other matters, the restructuring of chapter 2.) By 26 October, Lewis had completed and then "read over minutely" seventy thousand words of the typescript, telling Harcourt, "it strikes me as the real thing, with a good thick texture. As always it needs cutting—and will get it!"[23] And by 5 November, now in Rome, Lewis had finished ninety-five thousand words of the typescript "besides reading over, doing a little revision on, and making a lot of later-to-be-taken-up suggestions on the first 70,000 words."[24] He had finished the first draft and done some further revising by the end of February 1922. Lewis worked through the typescript several times during March and April, then typed up a clean copy of the revised draft before sailing back to New York on 13 May, completed manuscript in hand.

The clean typescript, which was probably used as setting copy, does not survive, but collation of the draft typescript and the first edition shows that Lewis did most of his revising on the draft. There are few sentences which he did not revise. Many of the changes are stylistic; with his characteristic meticulousness, Lewis tightened sentences, cut out prolixity, and paid great attention to diction even to the point of writing a list of three or four words then circling his final choice. Most of the substantive revisions, however, were done in the characterization of Babbitt. On one level, Lewis eliminated altogether or reduced the roles of several characters, evidently aiming to keep his focus on Babbitt. In chapter 6, for example, Babbitt was to have had a lengthy conversation with his father-in-law, Henry Thompson, as they drive to see Noel Ryland at the Zeeco Motor Car Company. In this passage, Thompson tells Babbitt a Horatio Alger version of his own life which Babbitt listens to with rapt attention (*Typescript*, pp. 97–8). And Babbitt's mother (called "Madame Babbitt") originally attended Babbitt's dinner party in chapter 9. Larger roles were also planned for Howard Littlefield and Sam Dopplebrau, Babbitt's next-door neighbors. Three scenes cancelled in the typescript suggest that Lewis intended to use them as counterweights to Babbitt, placing the main character more obviously between the extreme conservativism of Littlefield and the extreme liberalism of Doppelbrau (*Typescript*, pp. 14–15; 52; 90–91). Most interesting are the cuts involving the evangelist Mike Monday (a satirical version of Billy Sunday), who appears briefly in chapter 7 (pp. 98–100). At this point in the typescript, Lewis wrote an additional nine pages on Monday, "the world's greatest salesman of salvation" who has, "by efficient organization ... kept the overhead of spiritual regeneration down to an unprecedented rock-bottom basis" and converted "over two hundred thousand lost and priceless souls at an average cost of less than ten dollars a head" (*Typescript*, p. 138). Lewis possibly eliminated the Monday passages in anticipation of someday doing a "preacher novel"—*Elmer Gantry* (1927)—which he had considered before writing *Babbitt*. But it seems clear that in reducing the roles of these and other characters in the typescript, Lewis wanted to focus on Babbitt rather than on a certain set of people within or outside Babbitt's class.

Accordingly, Lewis made many revisions in the depiction of his central character. Herein lies the most interesting shift in Lewis' intentions. In a very few places, he softened the characterization of Babbitt, making him less exaggerated, less of a caricature. But in a greater number of places, mostly near the end of the typescript draft, Lewis deleted passages, often running to a dozen pages or more, which resulted in revisions of a different sort. In these deleted scenes Babbitt is more of a multi-dimensional character than he is in the published text—he is more realistic, more human.

Evidence of Lewis' softening Babbitt occurs mainly in the early chapters, particularly the original version of Babbitt's speech to the real estate board, which is harsher in typescript than it is in the published text. In his remarks about the "Ideal Citizen" as a churchgoer, for example, Babbitt is downright contemptuous of men who are not "modest, loyal Christians"; they do not "appreciate the fact that ... this country [is] a good place to live in and do business in—a land equally free of the insane hell-raising communistic maniacs and of the rotten irreligious voluptuaries that burden other lands" (*Typescript*, p. "F"). Elsewhere in the speech, Babbitt is equally vituperative about subjects that "threaten" America. In having Babbitt discuss literature, for example, Lewis indulged in various private jokes such as one in which Babbitt reacts against

> these hopeless literary groupies, these twenty-year-old know-it-alls, that go for one million dull sloppy pages describing every fly in the grocery stores on Main Street, or write about the love-affairs of a young socialistic pup, or the sad sorrows of kitchen mechanics, or about a place called "Winesburg" but it ought to be called "Coca-Cola Center"? (*Typescript*, p. "J")

Similarly, Babbitt's dire prophesies about "irresponsible teachers and professors, long-haired pups who work under cover" and concoct "nefarious plots to wreck the Constitution" present him as almost neurotic (*Typescript*, p. "N–A").

But by far the most revisions in the typescript worked in the opposite direction, for they deleted much material that made Babbitt a less clownish and a more fully-rounded character. These revisions occur mostly in the last third of the novel, as Babbitt flirts briefly with nonconformity. Very few of these passages are stylistically elegant or psychologically precise enough for Lewis to have kept them in the published text. It is clear why he deleted them, but the passages are significant in that they show Lewis trying to invest Babbitt's character with more self-knowledge than he ultimately has in the novel. Just as there is little sense in the published text of what drives Babbitt to rebel, there is equally little sense of how he feels about himself as he does so—at least there is less sense of this in the published text than there is in the typescript. In many deleted typescript passages, Lewis tried to show Babbitt's thinking as he questions his identity. In chapter 29, for instance, during the party held by "the Bunch" at Tanis Judique's apartment, Babbitt originally experienced this shock of vision:

> To Babbitt came that ancient sorrow of the man who discovers, as man forever is discovering, that in gilded and celebrated vice ... there is less joy than he had expected.... He crept off to the bathroom and drank much too much, and worried about his drinking while he did so, and hated himself rather spiritedly. (*Typescript*, pp. 277-C [477-C, misnumbered])

Yet in the published text, Babbitt's feelings are not described; he simply goes home, "fully a member of the Bunch" (p. 329). Similarly, Lewis removed two awkwardly written paragraphs from the end of chapter 23 which showed Babbitt alone in his house during his family's absence, "formlessly lonely as he lay on his cot on the sleeping porch, that night, his arms behind his head, the pillow poked and wadded, and he was naively young with the desire to be young" (*Typescript*, p. 386). Frequently Lewis deleted codas at the ends of chapters which he thought clumsy. At the end of typescript chapter 25, for instance, the conclusion of his Maine holiday without Paul Riesling, Babbitt vows to return to Zenith a new man, "at forty-seven, a frontiersman, renowned for his cynical humor, his original philosophy, and his quiet intimidating courage"—an ideal vision of himself—but all he can think of is the "scandal and loud murmur in Zenith" over his innocent flirtation with Ida Putiak, the manicurist, which haunts only Babbitt, for it exists exclusively "in the annals of the Babbitt family—for the sole absurd reason that they never happened in Babbitt's dream, which was so much more real than drudging reality" (*Typescript*, p. 418). Lewis cut this paragraph and wrote alongside it "Awk. Chap. ending." Awkward, to be sure, but also more ironic and less hackneyed than its replacement: "Thus it came to him [that] merely to run away was folly, because he could never run away from himself" (p. 300).

Elsewhere in the typescript, Lewis depicted Babbitt as more obviously trying to understand why his "standardized" life no longer satisfies him. At the end of typescript chapter 21, when Babbitt learns that Paul Riesling has shot his wife, Zilla, Lewis appended a sentence which does not appear in the first edition:

> He sat mechanically holding the telephone but hearing nothing; and he who had lived on the surface of life, a thing of shadow victories, purposeless hustlings, and thin desires, began to live below the surface, in a world turbulent, dark, and in its passion beautiful. (*Typescript*, p. 359)

This sentence foreshadows Babbitt's entry into a subterranean life of half-hearted bohemianism and shows us some of the emotions that compel him to do so. It is one of several attempts at a psychological probing of Babbitt's character that Lewis, it seems, could not polish sufficiently to use in the published text. Some cuts, such as this one, were evidently suggested by Grace, who read and commented upon the manuscript to Lewis as he worked on it in Italy. Along the bottom right-hand edge of this page, Grace wrote, "Troppo forte! Molto diminuendo! and drew a sketch of a figure that is unmistakeably Lewis with a pained expression on his face and his fingers pinching his nose. Lewis evidently agreed that the passage was too strong, or "loud," for he cancelled it in the typescript.

Some deleted passages seem to have been holdovers from the "plan," more detailed descriptions of Babbitt growing restless with his life and wanting to escape it. In chapter 27, Lewis originally had Babbitt confide to Myra his doubts about himself, a conversation occasioned by the ongoing labor unrest in Zenith:

> Ever since Paul—since that happened—I've felt a fellow oughtn't to jump at conclusions, and so on—see how I mean?—too soon. I don't—Oh, God, I don't know! I don't feel so cocksure about things as I used to.... Maybe I'm getting old.... But—Things don't seem as plain as they used to. All kind of black and white, that's how I used to see them. Even morals and that stuff. (*Typescript*, p. 445)

Here, Babbitt is unable to express himself, unable to frame his complex motivations in coherent language. That he cannot do so denies him self-knowledge. By contrast, in the published version of the passage Babbitt mildly questions public opinion about the strikers: "they're not such bad people. Just foolish" (p. 318). Missing are Babbitt's imperfect attempts at introspection and his fears that he may be losing his identity. In a deleted passage in chapter 19, after Babbitt fires Stanley Graff for his unethical behavior, Lewis showed Babbitt's inner humanity at war with his public facade:

> presently he forgot the horrible hour when he had awakened on the sleeping-porch at four in the morning, furious[ly] admitted Graff's charges, seen himself as a failure, wondered whether it was the Wheels of Progress that he had been propelling, and suddenly blasphemed, "Oh damn all these damn phrases! Damn all this damn booster stuff!! Damn the Wheels of Progress! Damn these High Endeavors!"
> (*Typescript*, p. 323)

This cut was also suggested by Grace; Lewis noted at the bottom of this page, "No says G—Bah growing neurotic as Carol [Kennicott]." Grace then wrote on the page: "Hear, hear; stop at 'as a son, I had much comfort in him,'" and Lewis accordingly deleted the passage at that point in the published text (p. 240). Grace's criticism is justified, but the passage also shows a Babbitt who is more aware of himself, yet woefully inept at articulating his thoughts.

In some of these deleted passages, Lewis tried to describe Babbitt's quest for self-knowledge in prose that was often top-heavy with tropes. In chapter 27, for example, when Vergil Gunch tries to coax Babbitt into explaining why he has seemed melancholy, Lewis originally described Babbitt as "conscious that his voice wasn't hearty enough," because "Fear, looming and gray, sat beside him. For two days he did not go to the club, but ate alone at a lunch-room on Washington Avenue; and Fear, vague, inexplicable, gray, and looming, lunched with him" (*Typescript*, p. 444). In the published text, the conversation between the two friends does not take place, and when Babbitt sees Gunch from across the street, Babbitt simply drives off (p. 318). Similarly, in other passages not included in the published novel we see Babbitt's desire to be young warring with his realization that he is essentially a Babbitt. One such passage occurs near the end of this same chapter, when Babbitt's fears about being rejected by the "Clan of Good Fellows" increasingly threaten him as word begins to spread of his affair with Tanis Judique. In the published version, the chapter ends with a matter-of-fact example of Babbitt's worries: "Could the fellows think I've gone nutty just because I'm broad-minded and liberal? Way Verg looked at me—" (p. 319). In the typescript there follows a cancelled passage in which the fairy girl of Babbitt's dreams in chapters 1 and 7 reappears:

> He forgot Tanis Judique, at the magic second when her image
> had almost merged with that of the fairy girl; he was restlessly
> and sharply awake, and in the night, behind the faintly seen
> elm, Fear sat silently watching. (*Typescript*, p. 447)

Here, Lewis makes concrete the suggestion that in pursuing Tanis, Babbitt is pursuing the concept of a woman, or of some form of escape, that he has been chasing for many nights of his life.

*   *   *   *

However imperfect these deleted passages are, they reveal that Lewis originally conceived his protagonist as less the figure that Mencken called the "Booboisie" and more of a multi-dimensional, human character. By cutting such material, Lewis at least partly reduced Babbitt's essential humanity—as he seems also to have done by rejecting the "plan." This is not to say that the Babbitt of the published novel has no intelligence or understanding of himself. However, since its publication, a commonplace criticism of the novel has been that Lewis did not succeed in creating a character of multiple dimensions, nor was he capable of producing a hero who would embody his notion of what was desirable in modern man. Even Stuart Pratt Sherman, in a promotional pamphlet on Lewis commissioned by Harcourt, Brace, and published just after *Babbitt*, had to admit that the novel would have been improved if Lewis had found some means (possibly through the other characters) of making Babbitt "more genuine" and "more inward" than he is, of imbuing him with some "social and personal felicity."[25] Less sympathetically, Frederick J. Hoffmann has concluded that "the crucial fact about *Babbitt* is that it is ... two types of literary exposition poorly combined in one work": there is a "limited" presentation of "a sensitive, humane Babbitt" whose validity is cancelled by "The parody Babbitt," whom Lewis was unable to humanize.[26] The characterization of Babbitt in the plan and the typescript suggests, however, that Lewis tried to create a character with more of a capacity for meaningful rebellion and change than we see in the published text.

The revisions also illustrate perhaps the biggest aesthetic problem that Lewis tried to work out as he wrote *Babbitt*—how to humanize a satirical character. Throughout the composition of the novel, Lewis repeatedly mentioned this problem. He told Harcourt and Donald Brace, Harcourt's partner, that he had "tried to make [Babbitt] human and ... not a type," but at the same time he wanted to create a character who "completely sums up certain things in all contemporary Babbitts."[27] On another occasion he wrote Harcourt, "I want utterly to develop [Babbitt] so that he will seem not just typical but an individual."[28] To Mencken he confided that he did not want Babbitt to be "merely burlesque"—"I've tried to make him human and individual, not a type."[29] This intention was motivated largely by reviews of *Main Street*, specifically one by Francis Hackett in *The New Republic* which claimed that Lewis could not go beyond stereotypes to create fully-developed characters. Lewis told Harcourt that Babbitt would "correct any faults of 'exterior vision,' of sacrifice of personality to types and environment" that Hackett had noted.[30]

Yet Lewis evidently had great difficulty in presenting Babbitt in this somewhat more sympathetic light. The reasons seem clear enough from the documentary evidence. Many of the deleted typescript passages suggest that Lewis was unable to find a suitable authorial voice with which to express Babbitt's feelings. Lewis attempted to fashion one which would be understanding toward Babbitt without being clumsy or hackneyed, or which went to the opposite extreme and presented a Babbitt who was neurotic—as Grace observed—or overly romanticized—as the diction in the deleted passages, with its somewhat belabored tropes, suggests. But Lewis could not create such a persona; so the only voice left him was an ironic one, the characteristic voice of the published novel.

Lewis also seems to have guarded carefully against making Babbitt a romanticized figure. In an early letter to Harcourt, Lewis said:

> I want the novel to be the G. A. N. [great American novel] in so far as it crystallizes and makes real the Average Capable American. No one has done it ... no one has even *touched* it except Booth Tarkington in *Turmoil* and *Magnificent Ambersons*; and he romanticizes away all bigness.[31]

Lewis may have feared losing the satirical edge to his novel and presenting a Babbitt who embodied neither of the two qualities Lewis tried to hold in delicate equipoise—the human Babbitt and the clownish Babbitt—but who was merely a romantic dreamer without any of the "bigness" that Lewis wanted him to have. However, the materials with which he created the novel all suggest that Lewis thought of Babbitt in a more sympathetic way than we see him in the published text and that Lewis believed there was more complexity to this American type than he ultimately portrayed.

NOTES

1. All illustrations from the manuscripts and notes for *Babbitt* are reprinted here with the kind permission of the Sinclair Lewis Estate, the copyright holder, and the Beinecke Rare Book and Manuscript and Library of Yale University. They are the property of the Beinecke Library.

2. Lewis to Harcourt, 28 December 1920, *From Main Street to Stockholm: Letters of Sinclair Lewis, 1919–1931*, ed. Harrison Smith (Harcourt, Brace, 1951), p. 59. Hereafter, references to this volume will be cited as *Letters*. The unpublished materials are catalogued at the Beinecke as follows: "Babbitt Notebook" and "Babbitt Plan," Lewis Papers, Box 155; typescript, Box 32. Wherever possible, I have cited page references parenthetically, with the exception of the "Babbitt Notebook," which is not paginated. All page references to *Babbitt* are to the Harcourt, Brace first edition of 1922.

Funding for this research was provided by the National Endowment for the Humanities and by The Citadel; I am grateful to both. All unpublished materials by Lewis are quoted here with the kind permission of the Officers of the Yale University Library and Mr. Paul Gitlin, Executor of the Lewis Estate.

3. Lewis to Harcourt, 27 October 1920; Harcourt to Lewis, 4 November 1920; Lewis to Harcourt, 11 November 1920 and 20 November 1920, *Letters*, pp. 39, 41–42, 47.

4. *Some Experiences* (privately printed, 1951), p. 83.

5. Lewis to Harcourt, 17 December 1920, *Letters*, p. 57.

6. Lewis to Harcourt, 16 February 1920, *Letters*, p. 61.

7. "Afterword," *Babbitt* (New American Library, 1961), pp, 320–21.

8. Wharton to Lewis, 27 August 1922, *The Letters of Edith Wharton*, eds. R.W.B. Lewis and Nancy Lewis (Scribner's, 1988), p. 455.

9. Lewis to Harcourt, 15 June 1921; 12 July 1921, *Letters*, pp. 72, 77.

10. One assumes that Lewis wrote a complete scenario for the novel and that only the seven and a half pages discussed here have survived. In her memoir, *With Love From Gracie: Sinclair Lewis, 1912–1925* (Harcourt, Brace, 1955), Grace speaks of a "synopsis of sixty thousand words," probably referring to the "plan" (p. 173).

11. See Harcourt to Lewis, 20 January 1922, *Letters*, p. 94. Harcourt worried about "giving away as much of your point of view as that speech does rather than having it grow out of the development of the characters as the reader goes along."

12. The last page of this fragment (p. 32), designated to be placed chronologically in "Jan 1921" of the novel, shows another change in focus: Lewis thought of having Will and Carol Kennicott, the central characters in *Main Street*, enter the novel. Will was to have been Babbitt's second cousin, visiting Zenith from Gopher Prairie. Lewis' notes read, "Ken's boasts re G.P. Contrast Bab and Ken", indicating that he would have used this material to examine further the evolution of the Midwestern city, for he intended to show ironically the two men "boosting" their hometowns—Babbitt having been conditioned to do so and Kennicott just becoming accustomed to such behavior.

13. Lewis to Mencken, "August 1921," quoted in Mark Schorer, *Sinclair Lewis: An American Life* (McGraw-Hill, 1961), pp. 290–91.

14. Harcourt may have been partly responsible for changing Lewis' thinking: after reading the first fifty-seven pages of the typescript, Harcourt suggested that Lewis "keep the whole book as the story of a man, and let it show what it will about big towns, small towns, or civilization, or any other damn thing" (Harcourt to Lewis, 13 February 1922, *Letters*, p. 99). Lewis, however, was worried that critics were anticipating Babbitt as another study of a place, such as *Main Street*. He, therefore, wrote Harcourt about "the need for sending out a note" to the press "about the new novel not being Zenith but *Babbitt*" (Lewis to Harcourt, 12 February 1922, *Letters*, p. 97).

15. *Sinclair Lewis* (Twayne, 1962), p. 85.

16. "The Revolt from the Village: 1920," *Nation*, CXIII (12 October 1921), p. 411.

17. "Portrait of an American Citizen," *Smart Set*, LXIX (October 1922), p. 139.

18. Grace Hegger Lewis to Ellen Eayres (Harcourt's secretary), 20 July 1921, *Letters*, p. 78.

19. Grace Hegger Lewis to Harcourt, 20 July 1921, *Letters*, pp. 78–9.

20. These drawings have been reprinted by Helen Batchelor as "A Sinclair Lewis Portfolio of Maps," *Modern Language Quarterly*, XXXII (1971), pp. 4111–7. They were discovered in 1961 in the former Lewis study at Twin Farms, the Barnard, Vermont, home in which he lived with his second wife, Dorothy Thompson. The maps are preserved among Thompson's papers at the George Arents Research Library of Syracuse University.

21. Lewis to Harcourt, 3 August 1921, *Letters*, p. 81.

22. Lewis to Harcourt, 18 October 1921, *Letters*, p. 85.

23. Lewis to Harcourt, 26 October 1921, *Letters*, p. 85.

24. Lewis to Harcourt, 5 November 1921, *Letters*, p. 87.

25. *The Significance of Sinclair Lewis* (Harcourt, Brace, 1922), p. 22.

26. *The Twenties: American Writing to the Postwar Decade* (Viking, 1955), p. 370.

27. Lewis to Harcourt and Brace, 20 January 1922, *Letters*, p. 95.

28. Lewis to Harcourt, 28 December 1920, *Letters*, p. 59.

29. Lewis to Mencken, "August 1921," in Schorer, p. 291.

30. Lewis to Harcourt, 30 November 1920, *Letters*, p. 52,

31. Lewis to Harcourt, 28 December 1920, *Letters*, p. 59.

Character Profile

Sinclair Lewis's *Babbitt* depicts the economic and cultural landscape of the fictional town of Zenith using a satirical slant and a sharp eye for detail. The book's eponymous character, George F. Babbitt, is a prototype of the 1920s' upstanding, prosperous middle-class citizen. Since conformity is indeed a high achievement in his realm, Babbitt's unremarkable qualities afford him complacency as he approaches middle age: "He was forty-six years old now, in April, 1920, and he made nothing in particular, neither butter nor shoes nor poetry, but he was nimble in the calling of selling houses for more than people could afford to pay."(2) Babbitt's looks, by the same token, are agreeable but by and large unremarkable. "His large head was pink, his brown hair thin and dry. His face was babyish in slumber, despite his wrinkles and the red spectacle-dents on the slopes of his nose. He was not fat but he was exceedingly well fed; his cheeks were pads, and the unroughened hand which lay helpless upon the khaki-colored blanket was slightly puffy."(2) Such a description is typical treatment by the narrator, who characterizes Babbitt through a scrim of social satire.

Like his neighbors and coworkers, Babbitt is concerned only with appearances and social standing. Power can be achieved only through possession, and Babbitt's world is ruled by the cultural divide that possessions create. There is a marked distinction, for example, between the Union Club—which boasts members of a slightly higher class, including the McKelveys—and the Athletic Club—where Babbitt and fellow boosters convene to exchange jokes and discuss their disdain for socialism, labor unions, and anarchy. Babbitt's appreciations of art, culture, ethics, and religion are largely without basis and cultivated only in order that he might win favor in his hypocritically high-minded crowd. The same is true of sport, as well: "He honestly believed that he loved baseball. It is true that he hadn't, in twenty-five years, himself played any baseball except back-lot catch with Ted—very gentle, and strictly limited to ten minutes. But the game was a custom of the clan, and it gave outlet for the homicidal and side-taking instincts which Babbitt called 'patriotism' and 'love of sport.'"(148) In almost all arenas, in fact, Babbitt's philosophies and value systems are full of unrealized and high-minded ideals and riddled with hypocrisy: "But Babbitt was virtuous," argues the narrator. "He advocated, though he did not practice, the prohibition of alcohol; he praised, though he did not obey, the laws against motor-speeding; he paid his debts; he contributed to the church, the Red Cross, and the Y.M.C.A.; he followed the custom of his clan and cheated only as it was sanctioned by precedent; and he never descended to trickery."(144) As a real estate broker and a writer of both ad copy and speeches, Babbitt defends his career's demands of hyperbole and occasional untruth by telling his best friend, Paul Riesling, "'And then most folks are so crooked themselves that they expect a fellow to do a little lying, so if I was fool enough to never whoop the ante I'd get the credit for lying anyway.'"

Despite such striving for self-satisfaction, Babbitt is secretly plagued by the notion that something is missing from his life. Desires that inspire action later in the novel begin needling him from the outset: "In twenty-three years of married life he had peered uneasily at every graceful ankle, every soft shoulder; in thought he had treasured them; but not once had he hazarded respectability by adventuring."(36) Paul Riesling helps bring some of this frustration to the fore—together the two men spend a week in Maine without the burdens of family or office. When they arrive, Babbitt murmurs, "'I'd just like to sit here—the rest of my life—and whittle—and sit. And never hear a typewriter. Or Stan Graft fussing in the 'phone. Or Rone and Ted scrapping. Just sit. Gosh!'"(143) Not so long after returning from this idyllic setting, Babbitt is shocked to catch his best friend involved in an extramarital affair, and eventually Paul ends up in jail for shooting his wife, Zilla, in the middle of an argument. His own needling questions made more painful by his friend's fall from grace, Babbitt rebels against the societal constraints he's worked so hard to follow. He begins a dalliance with the mature sophisticate and salon-leader Tanis Judique; in doing so he takes to drinking and becomes transfixed by her Bohemian circle of friends. Eventually the change that's come over him begets disdain and distance from his colleagues and Athletic Club friends—not so much for adultery as for the espousal of liberal politics and the outward support of his former schoolmate Seneca Doane, a radical lawyer and supporter of the labor movement. Soon enough this estrangement prompts Babbitt to doubt his own decisions, and when his wife Myra falls seriously ill he instantly realizes the folly of his actions. At the end of the novel, Babbitt returns to his place in the world with a slightly heightened awareness of the hypocritical ideology of his class. Though he may not have found the fulfillment he originally sought, he has made some progress. In the novel's closing scene, he blesses his son Ted's marriage to the movie-crazy Eunice Littlefield, and urges his son to avoid conforming to other people's expectations.

NOTE

All quotes are taken from the Signet Classic paperback version of *Babbitt*, copyright 1998.

Contributors

HAROLD BLOOM is Sterling Professor of the Humanities at Yale University and Henry W. and Albert A. Berg Professor of English at the New York University Graduate School. He is the author of over 20 books, including *Shelley's Mythmaking* (1959), *The Visionary Company* (1961), *Blake's Apocalypse* (1963), *Yeats* (1970), *A Map of Misreading* (1975), *Kabbalah and Criticism* (1975), *Agon: Toward a Theory of Revisionism* (1982), *The American Religion* (1992), *The Western Canon* (1994), and *Omens of Millennium: The Gnosis of Angels, Dreams, and Resurrection* (1996). *The Anxiety of Influence* (1973) sets forth Professor Bloom's provocative theory of the literary relationships between the great writers and their predecessors. His most recent books include *Shakespeare: The Invention of the Human* (1998), a 1998 National Book Award finalist, *How to Read and Why* (2000), *Genius: A Mosaic of One Hundred Exemplary Creative Minds* (2002), and *Hamlet: Poem Unlimited* (2003). In 1999, Professor Bloom received the prestigious American Academy of Arts and Letters Gold Medal for Criticism, and in 2002 he received the Catalonia International Prize.

RUSSELL AMES taught at Hunter College, City University of New York.

H.L. MENCKEN is considered one of the most prominent journalists, critics, and political commentators of his day. He is the author of *The American Language, Notes on Democracy, Treatise on Right and Wrong*, and *Happy Days*, among other works.

REBECCA WEST, English journalist, novelist, and critic, is perhaps best-known for her reports on the Nuremberg trials. She began her career as a columnist for the suffragist weekly, the *Freewoman*. She is also the author of *The Black Lamb and Grey Falcon*, *A Train of Powder*, and several novels, including *The Return of the Soldier*.

SHERWOOD ANDERSON made his name as a leading naturalistic writer with *Winesburg, Ohio*. In 1921 Anderson received the first *Dial* Award for his contribution to American literature. He is said to have encouraged William Faulkner and Ernest Hemingway in their writing aspirations.

STEPHEN S. CONROY is Associate Director of American Studies at the University of Florida and the author of essays on Emerson, Veblen, and Lewis as well as other works on American Popular culture.

DICK WAGENAAR has taught at Indiana University and is coauthor, along with Yoshio Iwamoto, of "The Last Sad Sigh: Time and Kawabata's *The Master of Go*."

BEA KNODEL is a Professor Emerita of English at St. Benedict's Monastery.

DAVID G. PUGH is author of several books and articles on masculinity and culture, including *The Masculine Mind in Nineteenth-Century America* and "History as an Expediant Accomodation: The Manliness Ethos in Modern America."

GORE VIDAL is a critic, essayist, and fiction writer. His first novel, *Williwaw* (1946), was based on his experiences in World War II. His best-known novel, *Myra Breckenridge* (1968), is a witty satire about a man who dies and returns to life as a woman. He also writes murder mysteries under the name Edgar Box.

JAMES M. HUTCHISSON is a Professor of English at The Citadel. In addition to three books on Sinclair Lewis, he is the author of *Perspectives on the Charleston Renaissance, 1920–40* and *DuBose Heyward: A Charleston Gentleman and The World of Porgy and Bess*.

Bibliography

Adams, J. Donald. "Speaking of Books." *New York Times Book Review* (July 31, 1960): 2.

Ames, Russell. "Sinclair Lewis Again." College English 10, Issue 2 (Nov., 1948): 77–80.

Anderson, David D. "Sinclair Lewis and the Nobel Prize." *MidAmerica* 8 (1981): 9–21.

Anderson, Sherwood. "Four American Impressions." *New Republic* 32 (1922): 172–173.

Austin, Allen. "An Interview with Sinclair Lewis." *University of Kansas City Review* 24 (1958): 199–210.

Babcock, C. Merton. "Americanisms in the Novels of Sinclair Lewis." *American Speech*, 35 (May 1960): 110–116.

Bucco, Martin. "Sinclair Lewis and 'The Greatest American Novelist.'" *Willa Cather Pioneer Memorial Newsletter* 29.1 (1985): 3–4.

Bucco, Martin, ed. *Critical Essays on Sinclair Lewis*. Boston: G.K. Hall & Co., 1986.

Bunge, Nancy L. "The Midwestern Novel: Walt Whitman Transplanted." *Old Northwest* 3 (1977): 275–287.

Calverton, V.F. "Sinclair Lewis, the Last of the Literary Liberals." *Modern Monthly* 8 (March 1934): 77–86.

Compton, Ida L., *Sinclair Lewis at Thorvale Farm: A Personal Memoir.* Sarasota: Ruggles Publishing, 1988.

Connaughton, Michael. Ed. *Sinclair Lewis at 100: Papers Presented at a Centennial Conference*. St. Cloud: St. Cloud State University Press, 1985.

Conroy, Stephen S. "Sinclair Lewis's Sociological Imagination." *American Literature* 42, Issue 3 (Nov., 1970): 348–362.

Corad, Robert L. "Edith Wharton's Influence on Sinclair Lewis." *Modern Fiction Studies* 31 (1985): 511–527.

———. "Jack London's Influence on Sinclair Lewis." *Sinclair Lewis at 100: Papers Presented at a Centennial Conference*. Ed. Michael Connaughton. St. Cloud: St. Cloud State University, 1985. 157–170.

Cypert, Rick. "Intellectuals, Introverts, and Cranks: What the Misfits Tell Us About Small-Town Life." *Markham Review* 16 (1986): 3–7.

Davidson, Richard Allan. "Sinclair Lewis, Charles G. Norris, and Kathleen Norris: An Early Friendship." *Modern Fiction Studies* 31 (1985): 503–510.

Dooley, D.J. *The Art of Sinclair Lewis*. Lincoln: University of Nebraska Press, 1967.

Dupree, Ellen Phillips. "Wharton, Lewis, and the Nobel Prize Address." *American Literature* 56 (1984): 262–270.

Fisher, Joel. "Sinclair Lewis and the Diagnostic Novel: Main Street and Babbitt." *Journal of American Studies* 20 (1986): 421–433.

Fleming, Robert E. "Recent Research on Sinclair Lewis." *Modern Fiction Studies*, 31.3 (Autumn 1985): 609–616.

Fleming, Robert E. and Esther. *Sinclair Lewis, a Reference Guide*. Boston: G.K. Hall, 1980.

Foster, Ruel E. "Lewis's Irony—A Paralysis of the Heart." *West Virginia University Philological Papers* 33 (1987): 31–40.

Gale, Robert L. "Lewis' Babbitt." *Explicator* 39.3 (1981): 39–40.

Geismar, Maxwell. *The Last of the Provincials: The American Novel, 1915–1925. H.L. Mencken, Sinclair Lewis, Willa Cather, Sherwood Anderson, F. Scott Fitzgerald*. London: Secker & Warburg, 1947.

———. "Sinclair Lewis: Forgotten Hero." *Saturday Review* 33 (June 25, 1960), 29–30.

Grebstein, Sheldom Norman. *Sinclair Lewis*. New York: Twayne, 1962

———. "Sinclair Lewis in Retrospect." *Gazette of the Grolier Club* N.S. 37 (1985): 35–44.

Hersey, John. "First Job." *Yale Review* 76.2 (1987): 184–197.

Hutchisson, James M. "'All of Us Americans at 46': The Making of Sinclair Lewis' *Babbitt*." *Journal of Modern Literature* 18, no.1 (1992): 95–114.

———. *The Rise of Sinclair Lewis, 1920–1930*. University Park: Pennsylvania State University Press, 1996.

———. "'Babbitt in Overalls': Sinclair Lewis' Abandoned Labor Novel." *South Dakota Review*, 29.4 (Winter 1991): 5–22.

Karlfeldt, Erik A., and Naboth Hedin. *Why Sinclair Lewis got the Nobel Prize*. New York: Harcourt, Brace and Company, 1931.

Knodel, Bea. "For Better or For Worse." *Modern Fiction Studies* 31, Issue 3 (1985): 555–563.

Koblas, John J. *Sinclair Lewis: Home at Last*. Bloomington, Minnesota: Voyageur Press, 1981.

Light, Martin. *The Quixotic Vision of Sinclair Lewis*. West Lafayette, Indiana: Purdue University Press, 1975.

———. Introduction to Sinclair Lewis: Special Issue. *Modern Fiction Studies* 31 (1985): 479–493.

Love, Glen A. *Babbitt: An American Life*. New York: Twayne, 1993.

Lundquist, James. *Sinclair Lewis*. New York: Ungar, 1972, 1973.

Manfred, Frederick. "Memories of Sinclair Lewis." *Gazette of the Grolier Club* 37 (1985): 21–34.

McLaughlin, Robert L. "'Only Kind Thing Is Silence': Ernest Hemingway vs. Sinclair Lewis." *Hemingway Review*, 6.2 (Spring 1987): 46–53.

Measell, James S. "A Descriptive Catalogue of Sinclair Lewis Novels." *SLN* 7–8 (1975–1976): 2–5.

Nevius, Blake. *The American Novel: Sinclair Lewis to the Present*. New York: Appleton-Century-Crofts, 1971.

O'Connor, Richard. *Sinclair Lewis*, American Writers Series. New York: Frederick Ungar, 1973.

Parry, Sally E. "The Changing Fictional Faces of Sinclair Lewis' Wives." *Studies in American Fiction* 17.1 (Spring 1989): 65–79.

———. "Gopher Prairie, Zenith, and Grand Republic: Nice Places to Visit, but Would Even Sinclair Lewis Want to Live There?" *Midwestern Miscellany* 20 (1992): 15–27.

Reitinger, D.W. "A Source for Tanis Judique in Sinclair Lewis's *Babbitt*." *Notes on Contemporary Literature* 23.5 (1993): 3–4.

Schorer, Mark. *Sinclair Lewis: An American Life*. New York: McGraw-Hill, 1961.

———. *Sinclair Lewis, a Collection of Critical Essays*. Englewood Cliffs, New Jersey: Prentice-Hall, 1962.

Sherman, Stuart P. *The Significance of Sinclair Lewis*. New York: Harcourt, Brace, 1922.

Town, Caren J. "A Dream More Romantic: Babbitt and Narrative Discontinuity." *West Virginia University Philological* Papers 33 (1987): 41–49.

Tuttleton, James W. Introduction. *Selected Short Stories of Sinclair Lewis*. Chicago: Ivan R. Dee, 1990.

Vidal, Gore. "The Romance of Sinclair Lewis." *The New York Review of Books*, October 8, 1992.

Watts, Emily Stipes. *The Businessman in American Literature*. Athens: University of Georgia Press, 1982.

Wilson, Christopher. "Sinclair Lewis and the Passing of Capitalism." *American Studies* 24.2 (Fall 1983): 95–108.

Young, Stephen A. "The Mencken-Lewis Connection." *Menckeniana* 94 (1985): 10–16.

Acknowledgments

"Sinclair Lewis Again," by Russell Ames. *College English* 10, No. 2 (November 1948): 77–80. © 1948 by the National Council of Teachers of English. Reprinted with permission.

"Portrait of an American Citizen," by H.L. Mencken. From *Sinclair Lewis: A Collection of Critical Essays*, edited by Mark Shorer: 20–22. © 1962 by Prentice Hall, Inc. Reprinted with permission.

"Babbitt," by Rebecca West. From *Sinclair Lewis: A Collection of Critical Essays*, edited by Mark Shorer: 23–26. © 1962 by Prentice Hall, Inc. Reprinted with permission.

"Sinclair Lewis," by Sherwood Anderson. From *Sinclair Lewis: A Collection of Critical Essays*, edited by Mark Shorer: 27–28. © 1962 by Prentice Hall, Inc. Reprinted with permission.

Stephen S. Conroy, "Sinclair Lewis's Sociological Imagination," in *American Literature*, Volume 42, No. 3, pp. 348–362. Copyright © 1970, Duke University Press. All rights reserved. Used by permission of the publisher.

Dick Wagenaar, "The Knight and the Pioneer: Europe and America and the Fiction of Sinclair Lewis," in *American Literature*, Volume 50, No. 2, pp. 230–249. Copyright © 1978, Duke University Press. All rights reserved. Used by permission of the publisher.

"For Better or Worse…" by Bea Knodel. *Modern Fiction Studies* 31, no. 3 (1985): 555–563. © 1985 by the Purdue Research Foundation. Reprinted with permission.

"Baedekers, Babbittry, and Baudelaire," by David G. Pugh. From *Critical Essays on Sinclair Lewis*, edited by Martin Bucco: 204–213. © 1986, G.K. Hall. Reprinted by permission of the Gale Group.

"The Romance of Sinclair Lewis," by Gore Vidal. *The New York Review of Books* (October 8, 1992). © 1992 NYREV, Inc. Reprinted with permission from *The New York Review of Books*.

"'All of Us Americans at 46': The Making of Sinclair Lewis' *Babbitt*," by James M. Hutchisson. *The Journal of Modern Literature* 18, no. 1 (Winter 1992): 95–114. © 1994 Temple University. Reprinted with permission.

Index